DIE GLOCKE
UNCOVERING THE NAZI BELL

SEBASTIAN THORN

Part I: The Roots of the Bell

Chapter 1: A Shadow in the Reich

In the final years of the Second World War, as the Allies closed in on Berlin from both East and West, a different kind of battle was taking shape—one not fought with rifles or tanks, but with blueprints, formulas, and terrifying ambition. Deep in the heart of the crumbling Reich, away from the bomb-blasted cities and bloodied frontlines, the Nazis were building shadows—devices and technologies so advanced they bordered on the mythic. Among them was a project so secretive, so shrouded in mystery, that its mere mention would vanish from the postwar record for decades. The project's name was *Die Glocke*. The Bell.

But before we can understand *Die Glocke*, we must first understand the world that birthed it—a world of *Wunderwaffe*, of desperate science, and of a regime willing to suspend reality in pursuit of ultimate power.

The Promise of Wunderwaffe

To a regime obsessed with symbolism and spectacle, the term *Wunderwaffe*—"wonder weapon"—was more than propaganda. It was a lifeline. As early as 1943, when it became clear that the Wehrmacht was overextended and faltering on both the Eastern and Western fronts, Nazi leadership turned increasingly toward the idea that a single, devastating technological breakthrough could reverse their fortunes.

These weapons were not mere upgrades to conventional arms. They were radical leaps: the *V-1* flying bomb, the first cruise missile; the *V-2* rocket, the world's first ballistic missile capable of striking London from occupied Europe; and the unfinished *V-3*, a multi-chambered "super gun" designed to fire shells into England from the French coast.

But behind these high-profile weapons lay a deeper, darker layer of research—projects buried in mountains, hidden in mine shafts, or erased entirely from record. These were the "black projects" of the Reich: secretive, compartmentalized efforts driven by desperation and divorced from conventional science. Here, the laws of physics were not guidelines—they were obstacles to be overcome.

The Rise of Kammler and the Black Programs

At the heart of many of these hidden programs stood one of the most elusive and powerful figures of the Third Reich: **SS General Hans Kammler**. An engineer by training and a bureaucrat by temperament, Kammler's early career was soaked in blood—he helped design the gas chambers and crematoria of Auschwitz. But in the war's final phase, his role shifted dramatically. Hitler, frustrated with the pace and inefficiency of his armaments ministry, handed Kammler control of advanced weapons programs, including the V-2 rocket.

Kammler, coldly efficient and ruthlessly secretive, created an empire of classified research that even the SS struggled to monitor. With access to enormous budgets, enslaved labor from concentration camps, and deep underground facilities, Kammler carved out a technological shadow state. He answered to no one, and his power grew unchecked.

It was within this shadow that *Die Glocke* may have been born.

The Hidden Infrastructure of the Occult Reich

The Nazis understood the value of secrecy, and nowhere was this more apparent than in their physical infrastructure. As Allied bombers leveled city after city, the Third Reich dug deep—literally. Vast tunnel systems were bored into mountainsides in places like the Harz and Owl Mountains. One such location was the **Wenceslas Mine**, in Lower Silesia (now Poland), a site tied by multiple researchers to the *Die Glocke* project.

Facilities like **Mittelwerk**, where V-2s were assembled by emaciated laborers under the earth, were designed not only to protect from bombs, but to hide what was truly being built. In many cases, the very existence of these installations was unknown to the majority of the German military.

And while physics and engineering were at the core of these efforts, so too were stranger pursuits. Hitler, Himmler, and many within the Nazi hierarchy were captivated by the idea that ancient knowledge—forgotten energy sources, lost civilizations, even time travel—might hold the key to Germany's salvation. The SS-funded **Ahnenerbe**, a pseudo-archaeological institute, sent expeditions to Tibet, the Arctic, and the Middle East in search of artifacts and esoteric knowledge. Their belief: that science and the supernatural could be fused to create weapons beyond imagination.

In this atmosphere of scientific hubris and mythic ambition, projects like *Die Glocke*—if real—seemed almost inevitable.

Whispers of the Bell

What is known of *Die Glocke* comes not from official war records, but from postwar investigations, obscure testimonies, and researchers piecing together fragments of a jigsaw puzzle scattered across continents.

Polish journalist **Igor Witkowski** would later claim to have uncovered references to the Bell in classified Polish intelligence documents. According to his findings, *Die Glocke* was a bell-shaped device, approximately 2.7 meters high and 1.5 meters in diameter, made of a heavy metal and filled with a strange, violet-hued substance code-named **Xerum 525**. It emitted radiation, reportedly killed several scientists during testing, and may have possessed anti-gravity or time-distorting capabilities.

But in 1945, as the Soviets advanced into Silesia, the Bell vanished. So did Kammler. Some say he was captured by the Americans. Others believe he was executed to ensure his secrets died with him. Still others insist he survived—and took *Die Glocke* with him, possibly to Argentina or even the United States under the cloak of **Operation Paperclip**.

A Beginning in Shadows

The truth about *Die Glocke* remains maddeningly elusive. Was it a real project? A myth? A misunderstood piece of conventional technology exaggerated by time and imagination? Or was it something far more dangerous—evidence that the Nazi war machine came closer to breaking the fabric of reality than we've dared admit?

This book is not an answer to those questions. It is an investigation. A reckoning. An attempt to trace the outline of the shadow cast by *Die Glocke*—a shadow born in the twilight of a dying Reich, in cold concrete bunkers lit by the flicker of failing lightbulbs and the fevered hopes of men who dreamed of rewriting the laws of nature.

In the chapters that follow, we will travel deeper into the labyrinth—through declassified files, forgotten mine shafts, strange testimonies, and unholy marriages of science and myth. Whether we emerge with answers or only deeper mysteries remains to be seen.

But this much is certain: the bell *did* toll. Somewhere in the Reich, in its final, crumbling days, it rang—and the echoes of its sound still haunt the corridors of forbidden science.

Chapter 2: The Ahnenerbe Agenda – Occult and Esoteric Underpinnings of Nazi Science

"We must find the keys to the ancient knowledge of our ancestors. In it lies the power to shape the world."
— Heinrich Himmler (allegedly, 1938)

Introduction: Where Myth Meets State

Among the many grotesque contradictions of the Nazi regime, perhaps none is more bizarre than its embrace of mysticism alongside cutting-edge science. While the Reich was home to brilliant minds like Wernher von Braun and built the first operational ballistic missile, it also spent enormous resources searching for the **Holy Grail**, deciphering **Runic inscriptions**, and sending expeditions to **Tibet** in search of the mythical **Aryan homeland**.

At the center of this dark fusion of **myth, mysticism, and pseudoscience** stood a little-known but powerful organization: the **Ahnenerbe**.

Founded in 1935, the Ahnenerbe was not just a cultural research institute—it was the **occult think tank of the SS**, designed to unearth what its leaders believed was **ancient, forgotten power** that once belonged to the Germanic peoples. By reviving and mastering this hidden knowledge, the Nazis hoped to legitimize their racial ideology, develop new technologies, and perhaps even unlock supernatural forces.

This chapter explores the **Ahnenerbe Agenda**: how pseudoscience and the occult were institutionalized within Nazi Germany—and how this ideology created fertile ground for projects like *Die Glocke*.

---

1. The Founding of the Ahnenerbe

The **Ahnenerbe** (short for *"Deutsches Ahnenerbe – Studiengesellschaft für Geistesurgeschichte, Deutsches Erbe"*, or "Ancestral Heritage Research and Teaching Society") was founded by **Heinrich Himmler, Herman Wirth, and Richard Walther Darré**.

Himmler, the head of the SS and perhaps the most ideologically extreme of the Nazi high command, believed in a mythic prehistory where an ancient, Nordic-Aryan race once ruled the Earth with wisdom and technological prowess. He saw Christianity as a Jewish corruption of ancient Germanic paganism, and sought to revive a **"pure" pagan-Aryan worldview**.

The Ahnenerbe was tasked with "proving" these beliefs through pseudo-archaeological, anthropological, and historical research. But their true agenda was always ideological: to **invent a heroic, mythic past** that would justify the racial, territorial, and metaphysical ambitions of the Nazi state.

---

2. Missions and Mysticism: The Work of the Ahnenerbe

The Ahnenerbe was involved in more than 50 expeditions and projects, many of which blurred the lines between scholarship, propaganda, and esoterica.

A. Tibetan Expedition (1938–1939)

- Led by zoologist **Ernst Schäfer**, this mission sought evidence that Tibet was a cradle of the Aryan race.
- The team collected **skulls, cultural artifacts**, and **religious texts**, believing Tibetan culture preserved echoes of ancient Aryan knowledge.
- The expedition helped fuel the belief that **Shambhala** or **Agartha**—mythical underground realms of wisdom—were real, and may have contained forgotten energy sources or lost technologies.

References:

- *Christopher Hale, "Himmler's Crusade: The Nazi Expedition to Find the Origins of the Aryan Race" (2003)*

B. The Externsteine and German Sacred Geography

- The Ahnenerbe conducted studies at **Externsteine**, a group of sandstone pillars in Westphalia believed by Himmler to be a prehistoric Aryan religious site.
- They believed the rocks were aligned with celestial events, linking them to **sun worship**, **rune magic**, and ancient "cosmic science."

C. Grail Quests and Arthurian Myths

- Himmler's obsession with the **Holy Grail**, inspired by Wagner's *Parsifal*, led to investigations into medieval German epics like the **Nibelungenlied**.
- SS officer **Otto Rahn**, an Ahnenerbe affiliate, sought the Grail in southern France, connecting Cathar ruins with hidden relics.

References:

- *Michael Baigent, Richard Leigh, and Henry Lincoln, "Holy Blood, Holy Grail" (1982)*

---

3. Pseudoscience as State Policy

The Ahnenerbe was not merely symbolic. It shaped **policy, racial ideology**, and even **military strategy** through its influence on SS leadership.

A. Racial Anthropology and Eugenics

- The Ahnenerbe conducted skull measurements, genetic studies, and other anthropological experiments to "prove" Aryan superiority.
- This included **cruel human experiments** in concentration camps under the guise of racial science.

B. Germanic Revivalism

- The SS sought to reconstruct a **pagan Aryan religion**, using Ahnenerbe research to develop rituals, holidays, and symbols.

- The **Wewelsburg Castle**, redesigned by Himmler as an SS "Camelot," was steeped in Ahnenerbe symbology and was intended as the spiritual center of a new Aryan empire.

C. Energy and Earth Mysteries

- The Ahnenerbe encouraged study into **earth energies**, **ley lines**, **magnetism**, and other fringe physics—believing ancient peoples had knowledge of "natural forces" long lost to modern science.
- These ideas would resonate with later reports of exotic Nazi technologies like **Die Glocke**, which was rumored to manipulate gravity, time, or energy fields.

4. The Road to Die Glocke

While no direct documentation links the Ahnenerbe to *Die Glocke*, the philosophical groundwork is undeniable.

The Ahnenerbe popularized the idea that **ancient wisdom**, **cosmic forces**, and **technological power** were not mutually exclusive—but deeply intertwined. This worldview made the pursuit of devices like the Bell, rumored to generate anti-gravity effects or temporal anomalies, **ideologically acceptable**, even **desirable**, to high-ranking Nazis.

- **Kammler's secretive SS research divisions** absorbed Ahnenerbe personnel and influence.
- Projects like *Die Glocke* may have been hybrids—part advanced physics, part esoteric engineering.
- The **symbolism** of the Bell (a recurring religious and alchemical motif) suggests deliberate occult associations.

5. Collapse and Erasure

As the Third Reich collapsed, so too did the Ahnenerbe. Many documents were destroyed; many members disappeared or were absorbed into postwar programs.

- Some Ahnenerbe-affiliated scientists were recruited by the **U.S. (Operation Paperclip)** and **Soviet Union**.
- Others were tried at Nuremberg for war crimes due to their role in human experimentation.

Yet their **ideological legacy** survived in strange ways—feeding **postwar myths, conspiracy theories**, and **claims of hidden Nazi technologies** in Antarctica, South America, and beyond.

The Ahnenerbe represents the most extreme case of **myth weaponized as policy**. It was not a fringe cult on the edges of the Nazi regime—it was *in the bloodstream*, influencing some of its most powerful men and darkest crimes.

Without the Ahnenerbe, it is unlikely that *Die Glocke*—a device that defies conventional categorization—would have been conceived. For within the Ahnenerbe's warped logic, such a project made perfect sense: a fusion of forgotten wisdom, cutting-edge science, and the belief that man could seize the power of the gods.

In the next chapter, we descend further into this world—into the mountains and mines where these dreams took form in metal, stone, and silence.

Suggested References and Further Reading:

1. **Christopher Hale**, *Himmler's Crusade: The Nazi Expedition to Find the Origins of the Aryan Race* (2003)
2. **Michael Baigent et al.**, *Holy Blood, Holy Grail* (1982)
3. **Heather Pringle**, *The Master Plan: Himmler's Scholars and the Holocaust* (2006)
4. **Nicholas Goodrick-Clarke**, *Occult Roots of Nazism* (1985)
5. **Peter Levenda**, *Unholy Alliance: A History of Nazi Involvement with the Occult* (1995)

Chapter 3: Kammler's Empire – The Rise of SS General Hans Kammler and His Hidden Projects

"Kammler was the most powerful man in Germany that nobody ever heard of."
— U.S. Army Intelligence Report, 1946 (classified)

Introduction: The Architect of Shadows

As the Allied forces closed in on Berlin in the final months of World War II, one man quietly disappeared from the ruins of the Third Reich. His name was **Hans Kammler**, an SS General with no battlefield glory, no public presence, and no postwar obituary. Yet in the final phase of the war, Kammler had more control over Nazi Germany's most advanced and secretive weapons programs than any other individual.

He was the **master builder** of Auschwitz's crematoria, the **administrator of the V-2 rocket program**, and—according to several postwar sources—the overseer of **Die Glocke**, the so-called Nazi Bell. His reach extended across a vast hidden empire of underground tunnels, advanced laboratories, and enslaved labor.

Kammler's story is not just about power—it's about the transformation of Nazi science from battlefield innovation to **black project secrecy**, and about a man who vanished into history with some of its darkest secrets.

1. From Bureaucrat to Butcher

Hans Kammler was born in 1901 in Stettin, Prussia (modern-day Szczecin, Poland). Trained as a civil engineer, he earned a doctorate in engineering and joined the **Nazi Party** in 1931, followed by the **SS** in 1933. His technical mind and bureaucratic skill made him a valuable asset to the growing Nazi apparatus.

During the 1930s, Kammler worked in the **Reich Ministry of Construction**, helping design military and administrative infrastructure. But his most notorious assignment came in the early 1940s, when he was appointed to oversee the design and construction of **concentration and extermination**

camps, including the gas chambers and crematoria at **Auschwitz-Birkenau**.

Kammler was not a scientist or soldier—he was a **manager of death**, with a gift for organizing mass-scale operations with cold efficiency. His skill at organizing human suffering would later be redirected toward organizing technological development on a massive, secretive scale.

---

2. Rocketman of the Reich: Taking Over Peenemünde

By 1943, the Nazi leadership grew increasingly frustrated with the **V-2 rocket program**, led by **Wernher von Braun** at Peenemünde. Though promising, the project suffered from delays, internal conflicts, and vulnerability to Allied bombing.

In September 1944, Himmler placed Hans Kammler in charge of the V-2 program. Kammler's solution was brutal and efficient:

- He **moved production** of the rockets underground to the **Mittelwerk tunnels** near Nordhausen in the Harz Mountains.
- He used **forced labor** from the adjacent **Mittelbau-Dora concentration camp**, resulting in the deaths of an estimated **20,000 prisoners**, many more than the V-2 rockets ever killed in combat.

Kammler was now in charge of the **world's first ballistic missile**, and he ran it like a totalitarian corporation—tight secrecy, brutal discipline, and zero tolerance for failure.

Reference:

- Michael J. Neufeld, *The Rocket and the Reich* (1995)
- André Sellier, *A History of the Dora Camp* (2003)

---

3. Empire Underground: Kammler's Network of Black Sites

Kammler's empire expanded rapidly in 1944–1945. With Hitler and Himmler's full backing, he became the de facto **czar of Nazi black projects**. His power extended across a shadowy web of secret installations, most hidden in subterranean or mountainous regions.

Key Sites Under Kammler's Command:

- **Mittelwerk (Nordhausen)** – V-2 production tunnels
- **Ebensee (Austria)** – Underground lab for high-tech research
- **Jonastal (Thuringia)** – Alleged command bunker or research site
- **Wenceslas Mine (Ludwikowice Kłodzkie, Poland)** – Allegedly tied to *Die Glocke*
- **Project Riese (Owl Mountains, Poland)** – A vast and mysterious complex of tunnels and chambers, purpose still debated

These facilities were constructed by the **Organisation Todt** and SS engineering units, often using thousands of slave laborers. Many were never completed, but some housed operational labs where researchers worked on **jet engines, nuclear experiments, anti-gravity propulsion**, and other exotic ideas.

References:

- Igor Witkowski, *The Truth About the Wunderwaffe* (2003)
- Geoffrey Brooks, *Hitler's Terror Weapons* (2002)

4. Die Glocke and Exotic Physics

While no official wartime documentation directly connects Kammler to *Die Glocke*, postwar reports, including those from Polish and U.S. intelligence sources, suggest he was the ultimate authority behind the project.

According to journalist **Igor Witkowski**, who interviewed a former Polish intelligence officer, *Die Glocke* was a **bell-shaped device** housed at the Wenceslas Mine and powered by a mysterious substance called **Xerum 525**. The device reportedly emitted intense radiation, affected gravity, and may have had temporal or spatial effects.

Key elements allegedly linked to Kammler:

- All test personnel involved in the Bell project were allegedly executed by Kammler's order.

- The device was one of the few projects prioritized even in the final days of the war.
- Kammler reportedly disappeared with documents and possibly components related to *Die Glocke*.

References:

- Igor Witkowski, *The Truth About the Wunderwaffe*
- Nick Cook, *The Hunt for Zero Point* (2001)

---

5. The Final Days and Kammler's Disappearance

Kammler was last officially seen in **early May 1945**. What happened next is the subject of **ongoing mystery and speculation**.

Official Nazi Version:

- Kammler committed suicide on **May 9, 1945**, in Czechoslovakia. His driver allegedly buried him by the roadside.
- No body was ever found, and his death certificate was filed *post facto* by SS comrades.

Alternative Theories:

- Kammler was **captured by American forces** and secretly transported to the U.S. under **Operation Paperclip**, like von Braun.
- He was **executed by the SS** to keep *Die Glocke* and other secrets from falling into Allied hands.
- He escaped to **South America**, perhaps with help from ODESSA or Vatican ratlines.

The U.S. Army's Counter Intelligence Corps (CIC) conducted multiple investigations into Kammler postwar. Declassified files show that they believed he was "of highest interest" due to his access to advanced technologies and scientists.

References:

- Joseph P. Farrell, *Reich of the Black Sun* (2004)

- Tom Agoston, *Blunder!: How the U.S. Gave Away Nazi Supersecrets to Russia* (1985)

6. Kammler's Legacy and the Birth of the Military-Industrial Complex

Whether Kammler died in 1945 or escaped into the Cold War shadows, his legacy endured. His system of **compartmentalized research**, **underground laboratories**, and **slave labor logistics** became a template for **postwar black operations** in both the U.S. and USSR.

- The **Paperclip scientists** who built America's space and missile programs—von Braun included—had all worked under Kammler.
- The **obsession with secrecy**, advanced propulsion, and physics-bending research echoed through **Area 51, Dulce Base myths**, and alleged **Nazi UFO programs**.

Kammler was more than a man—he was the architect of the world's first true **black budget weapons complex**, and his disappearance ensured that the full scope of his empire remains **unresolved, and deeply unnerving**.

Conclusion: The Man Who Knew Too Much

In a war defined by ideology, firepower, and genocide, Hans Kammler stands out not for his ideology or charisma, but for his **absolute control over secrecy and advanced technology**. He is the invisible hand behind the Nazi science that history has only begun to unravel.

He built the crematoria of Auschwitz and the V-2 rocket tunnels with equal detachment. He may have supervised a project—*Die Glocke*—that has baffled researchers for decades. And he vanished, like the technologies he oversaw, into the ether.

The story of Hans Kammler is not over. It remains a key to understanding what the Nazis left behind—not just machines, but an *infrastructure of secrecy* that shaped the modern world in ways still coming to light.

Suggested References and Further Reading:

1. Michael J. Neufeld – *The Rocket and the Reich* (1995)
2. Igor Witkowski – *The Truth About the Wunderwaffe* (2003)
3. Tom Agoston – *Blunder!* (1985)
4. Nick Cook – *The Hunt for Zero Point* (2001)
5. Joseph Farrell – *Reich of the Black Sun* (2004)
6. André Sellier – *A History of the Dora Camp* (2003)

Chapter 4: The Wenceslas Mine – Discovery and Development of the Mysterious Underground Facility in Lower Silesia

"A place where the boundaries of science and the supernatural were said to blur—buried beneath the forests of Silesia."
— Igor Witkowski, *The Truth About the Wunderwaffe* (2003)

Introduction: The Forgotten Mine

In the quiet countryside of **Lower Silesia**, now part of modern-day Poland, lies a disused industrial site. At first glance, the remnants appear unremarkable—collapsed concrete, moss-covered pillars, and rusted metalworks surrounded by trees. But for researchers of Nazi black projects and the elusive *Die Glocke*, this place is nothing short of a **Rosetta Stone of secrecy**.

Known today as the **Wenceslas Mine (or Wenceslaus Mine)**, this location is believed to have been one of the central test sites for Germany's most **esoteric wartime technology projects**. This includes the alleged construction and testing of *Die Glocke*, the so-called **Nazi Bell**—a device that may have involved anti-gravity, time distortion, or other unexplained phenomena.

While physical evidence remains scarce and much of the documentation has vanished, persistent investigative journalism, declassified intelligence, and site exploration have all pointed toward the Wenceslas Mine as a **critical node in the Nazi scientific underground**.

1. Geographic and Historical Context

Located near the village of **Ludwikowice Kłodzkie** (formerly **Ludwigsdorf**) in southwestern Poland, the Wenceslas Mine was originally a **coal and heavy industry facility**, operational in the late 19th and early 20th centuries.

Under Nazi occupation during World War II, the region became a hub for secret construction projects. The rugged, mountainous terrain of the **Owl Mountains (Góry Sowie)** made it ideal for hiding large underground facilities from Allied air raids.

Nearby sites, including **Project Riese** and **Książ Castle**, were also commandeered by the SS for clandestine research and military operations. The Wenceslas Mine was absorbed into this clandestine network—its industrial infrastructure retrofitted, expanded, and sealed under layers of secrecy.

References:

- Witkowski, Igor. *The Truth About the Wunderwaffe* (2003)
- Zaloga, Steven J. *Nazi Secret Weapons 1939–45* (2004)

2. Transformation into a Black Site

From 1943 onward, the Nazis accelerated the relocation of sensitive weapons research underground. With Allied bombing crippling surface facilities, the SS and **Organisation Todt** began hollowing out tunnels across Silesia. The Wenceslas Mine, already an industrial site with existing shafts and reinforced structures, was transformed.

Key developments included:

- **Reinforced concrete bunkers**: Added above and around test chambers.
- **Power infrastructure**: High-voltage power lines and massive generators were reportedly brought in—suggesting experiments requiring enormous energy input.

- **Rail connections and hidden access points**: Rail sidings into the forest and camouflaged access roads were developed to supply materials and personnel.
- **Slave labor**: Prisoners from **Gross-Rosen concentration camp** and its subcamps were forced to work in inhumane conditions.

While the mine's official use was listed as "research and manufacturing," local testimonies and postwar investigations suggest the work went far beyond conventional weapons development.

3. The Henge: A Concrete Mystery

At the center of the site lies the most mysterious structure of all: the **"Henge"**—a large concrete ring, approximately 30 feet in diameter, supported by thick vertical pillars arranged in a circle.

- Often referred to as a **"flytrap"**, the Henge is made of **reinforced concrete** and shows signs of electrical fittings or possibly pipe mounts.
- No other industrial use has ever been confirmed, and no documentation survives to explain its construction.
- The structure is **completely unique**—no known coal or chemical processing infrastructure from the era resembles it.

Some researchers, including Witkowski and aerospace journalist **Nick Cook**, believe this ring was a **support structure for testing Die Glocke**—possibly to suspend the device during operation or isolate it from ground contact.

Others argue it was part of a **cooling tower**, though no matching cooling infrastructure (piping, pumps, or reservoirs) has been found nearby.

References:

- Nick Cook, *The Hunt for Zero Point* (2001)
- Joseph P. Farrell, *Reich of the Black Sun* (2004)

4. Die Glocke: The Legend Begins Here

According to Witkowski's research, *Die Glocke* was tested here in **a deep underground chamber** connected to the mine complex. Codenamed **"Chronos"** or **"Laternenträger"** (Lantern Bearer), the Bell was allegedly:

- A metallic, bell-shaped device 2.7 meters tall and 1.5 meters in diameter
- Encased in **ceramic cladding** to protect from radiation
- Filled with a mysterious substance called **Xerum 525**, described as violet and mercury-like
- Powered by **extremely high-voltage electricity** and **rotating magnetic fields**

Tests allegedly resulted in:

- Deaths of numerous scientists and technicians due to **biological effects**
- Time or spatial anomalies, as claimed by some speculative accounts
- Movement of the device shortly before the war's end—possibly to Bavaria, Czechoslovakia, or even abroad

Witkowski's source, a retired **Polish intelligence officer**, claimed access to postwar interrogation records of German scientists and SS officers. These interviews allegedly linked *Die Glocke* to Kammler's command structure and the Wenceslas Mine.

---

5. Eyewitnesses, Silence, and Disinformation

Postwar interviews with local residents revealed eerie stories:

- Strange humming noises and blue lights at night
- Sudden disappearances of laborers and engineers
- German soldiers seen loading covered cargo onto trains in early 1945

However, most records of the Wenceslas site were either destroyed or seized. American and Soviet forces both advanced into the region within weeks of each other. The Soviet Army gained direct control over the area, and what happened next remains murky.

- **Soviet secrecy** enveloped the site postwar.
- No **official Allied report** has ever confirmed the Bell's existence.
- The **CIA** and **U.S. Army's G-2** division referenced "high-interest activity" in the Owl Mountains in several declassified documents—but without specific mention of *Die Glocke*.

This mixture of mystery, absence, and suggestive ruins has made the Wenceslas Mine a focal point for Nazi tech conspiracy theories ever since.

References:

- Declassified CIA Documents (FOIA Electronic Reading Room)
- Witkowski, *The Truth About the Wunderwaffe*

6. Modern Exploration and Interpretation

Today, the Wenceslas Mine is **accessible to the public**, though poorly marked and lacking official recognition. It draws curious researchers, conspiracy theorists, and tourists.

Key observations include:

- **Unexplained foundations** buried under the site
- Radioactivity levels in some areas slightly above background (though inconclusive)
- Remnants of **cabling, industrial ceramics**, and massive concrete slabs inconsistent with coal mining

Polish historical societies and independent archaeologists have conducted surveys but found no definitive proof of *Die Glocke*. Still, the structure's **unexplained design**, **strategic location**, and **proximity to other confirmed SS black sites** make it a compelling candidate for exotic experimentation.

Whether or not *Die Glocke* was ever tested here, the Wenceslas Mine represents something real: the **Nazis' immense investment in secret**

underground technology—the kind that required death, silence, and disappearing paper trails.

What happened here may remain buried, both literally and figuratively. But the site continues to draw attention because it sits at the **intersection of history, mystery, and mythology**. It is a physical place that raises metaphysical questions—about the nature of power, secrecy, and the price of progress pursued without morality.

As we continue our journey through Kammler's empire of shadows, the Wenceslas Mine reminds us that even the most fantastical legends often grow from real foundations.

Suggested References and Further Reading:

1. Igor Witkowski – *The Truth About the Wunderwaffe* (2003)
2. Nick Cook – *The Hunt for Zero Point* (2001)
3. Joseph P. Farrell – *Reich of the Black Sun* (2004)
4. Steven J. Zaloga – *Nazi Secret Weapons 1939–45* (Osprey Publishing)
5. Polish State Archives – Regional records from Wałbrzych and Kłodzko districts
6. Declassified CIA and OSS documents on Lower Silesian industrial activity (via FOIA)

Chapter 5: The Nazi Bell Emerges – First References to *Die Glocke* and Its Strange Properties

---

"It was code-named Die Glocke, and it was the most closely guarded secret of the Third Reich—more important even than the atomic bomb."
— Igor Witkowski, *The Truth About the Wunderwaffe* (2003)

Introduction: From Secrecy to Speculation

For decades after World War II, there was no mention of a device called *Die Glocke* in official records, military histories, or Allied intelligence files. It was not until the early 2000s that this strange, bell-shaped device began to capture the public imagination—thanks largely to the investigative work of a Polish journalist and military historian: **Igor Witkowski**.

According to Witkowski, *Die Glocke* was not a myth or fabrication, but a real and deadly experiment conducted under SS supervision in the final years of the war. Unlike the well-documented V-weapons or jet aircraft of the Third Reich, *Die Glocke* was part of an even deeper level of black project research—where science met the unknown.

In this chapter, we explore how the legend of *Die Glocke* emerged, the earliest references to it, and what is alleged about its construction, operation, and terrifying side effects.

---

1. The Witkowski Revelation

The first known reference to *Die Glocke* as a specific object comes from Polish author **Igor Witkowski**, in his 2000 book *Prawda o Wunderwaffe* (*The Truth About the Wunderwaffe*). In it, Witkowski claimed to have gained access to classified transcripts from a postwar Polish intelligence interview with a former high-ranking Nazi SS officer who had been involved in secret weapons projects.

The officer, whose identity was never publicly revealed, reportedly spoke at length about a mysterious device code-named **"Die Glocke"**—*The Bell*—which was tested at a secret installation in Lower Silesia, most likely the **Wenceslas Mine** near Ludwikowice Kłodzkie.

Witkowski described *Die Glocke* as:

- A **metallic bell-shaped object** approximately **2.7 meters high** and **1.5 meters wide**
- Composed of a **heavy, lead-like metal**, possibly wrapped in ceramic
- Suspended from a **gantry or support structure** (speculated to be the so-called **"Henge"**)
- Powered by **high-voltage electricity**, and containing two counter-rotating drums

Inside the device was a mysterious substance referred to as **Xerum 525**—described as a heavy, red-violet mercury-like compound, highly radioactive and stored in lead-lined containers.

---

2. Strange Effects and the Bell's Alleged Function

According to the testimony cited by Witkowski, and later echoed by other authors such as **Nick Cook**, the operation of *Die Glocke* produced **highly unusual and dangerous effects**:

Biological Impact

- Several scientists and technicians reportedly **died** during early tests.
- Animals exposed to the Bell's field experienced **crystalline breakdown** of tissues, **blood coagulation**, and **nervous system failure**—reminiscent of extreme radiation poisoning, yet different in cause.
- The device had to be operated in a **heavily shielded underground chamber**, and tests were conducted in short bursts.

Visual and Energetic Phenomena

- Witnesses described a **bluish or violet glow** surrounding the device during operation.
- Local civilians (according to anecdotal accounts) reported hearing **deep-frequency humming** and seeing **flickering lights** in the forest.

Space-Time Distortion?

- The most controversial claims involve the alleged **manipulation of gravity or time**.
- It was said that during operation, the Bell created **temporal effects**—a brief suspension or warping of time in the immediate vicinity.
- These claims have led to comparisons with theoretical **zero-point energy** research, **anti-gravity propulsion**, and even **time travel**.

References:

- Witkowski, Igor. *The Truth About the Wunderwaffe* (2003)

- Cook, Nick. *The Hunt for Zero Point* (2001)
- Farrell, Joseph P. *Reich of the Black Sun* (2004)

3. Code Names: Chronos and Laternenträger

The Bell was allegedly associated with two codenames:

- **Chronos** – The Greek word for time, hinting at the possible nature of the research.
- **Laternenträger** – "Lantern Bearer," an oddly poetic phrase that some have interpreted as symbolic, perhaps referring to the device's strange glow or occult overtones.

These codenames reinforce the idea that *Die Glocke* was not merely a weapon, but a device intended to explore **new domains of physical law**—perhaps even outside the bounds of standard wartime military logic.

4. Kammler's Role and Final Disappearance

According to both Witkowski and Cook, **SS General Hans Kammler** was the direct overseer of the Bell project. Known for running the V-2 program and controlling a network of underground facilities, Kammler allegedly ensured that *Die Glocke* remained **off the radar**, even from most of the Nazi high command.

Just days before the war ended, the Bell and all associated research were reportedly **moved or destroyed**. Some theories suggest:

- It was **buried or hidden** in Silesia, sealed in a shaft or tunnel.
- It was **evacuated by U-boat** and taken to **South America**.
- It was **captured by U.S. forces** and shipped back under **Operation Paperclip**.
- Kammler himself escaped with the technology, possibly negotiating with American intelligence for immunity.

No firm documentation has ever confirmed any of these theories, but Kammler's own **mysterious disappearance** adds fuel to the fire.

References:

- Agoston, Tom. *Blunder!: How the U.S. Gave Away Nazi Supersecrets to Russia* (1985)
- U.S. Army Counter Intelligence Corps (CIC) Reports, Declassified (NARA/FOIA)

---

5. The Kecksburg Incident and Postwar Parallels

Interest in *Die Glocke* surged again after comparisons were drawn between the Bell and the **Kecksburg UFO incident** of 1965 in Pennsylvania, USA.

In that incident:

- Witnesses saw a **bell-shaped object** crash into the woods.
- The object was reportedly **recovered by the U.S. military** and taken away under tight security.
- Eyewitnesses described **strange symbols** engraved around its base.

Several researchers, including **Joseph Farrell** and **Jim Marrs**, suggested that the Kecksburg object might have been *Die Glocke*—either **recovered postwar** or an **American version reverse-engineered** from Nazi research.

While the connection remains speculative, it demonstrates the **narrative potency** of the Bell story—it fuses **WWII secrecy**, **UFO mythology**, and **black project paranoia** into a single, persistent mystery.

---

6. Skepticism and Scientific Criticism

Mainstream historians and scientists have largely dismissed the Bell story as **conspiracy fiction** fueled by lack of evidence and sensationalist interpretation.

Critiques include:

- No surviving Nazi documents referencing "Die Glocke" by name
- Heavy reliance on **anonymous sources** and **third-hand intelligence**
- Alleged physical evidence (like the Henge) being **reinterpreted** as industrial infrastructure (e.g., a cooling tower base)

Yet the **absence of proof** does not eliminate the intrigue—especially given the **document destruction and secrecy** surrounding late-war SS projects.

Even critics admit that Nazi Germany was exploring **non-traditional energy research**, and that **Kammler's empire** of underground labs may still hold secrets.

Reference:

- Neufeld, Michael J. *The Rocket and the Reich* (1995)
- Goodrick-Clarke, Nicholas. *Black Sun: Aryan Cults, Esoteric Nazism and the Politics of Identity* (2002)

Whether real or imagined, *Die Glocke* symbolizes the **ultimate enigma of Nazi science**—a device said to straddle the line between physics and metaphysics, war and wonder, engineering and the occult.

Its first known references may have emerged only recently, but the conditions that gave rise to it—**esoteric ideology, black project secrecy, desperation, and brilliant madness**—are historically undeniable.

In the chapters ahead, we will explore what modern science makes of the Bell's alleged principles, and how its myth continues to echo in stories of UFOs, secret military research, and humanity's obsessive quest to control the forces of the universe.

Because somewhere between fact and fiction, the Bell still rings.

Suggested References and Further Reading

1. Igor Witkowski – *The Truth About the Wunderwaffe* (2003)
2. Nick Cook – *The Hunt for Zero Point* (2001)
3. Joseph P. Farrell – *Reich of the Black Sun* (2004)
4. Jim Marrs – *The Rise of the Fourth Reich* (2008)
5. Tom Agoston – *Blunder!* (1985)
6. FOIA/Declassified U.S. Intelligence Files on Nazi Advanced Weapons (NARA/CIA)

7. Michael J. Neufeld – *The Rocket and the Reich* (1995)

Part II: Technology Beyond Its Time

Chapter 6: Blueprints from Beyond – Alleged Technology, Design, and Structure of Die Glocke

"There is nothing in conventional engineering that even hints at such a device. The Bell—if it existed—was something entirely outside the known spectrum of science."
— Joseph P. Farrell, *Reich of the Black Sun* (2004)

Introduction: Engineering the Impossible

Among the many legends surrounding Nazi Germany's advanced weaponry programs, *Die Glocke* ("The Bell") stands apart—not merely for its secrecy, but for the boldness of its alleged design. This device, if real, was no conventional machine. It was said to operate on principles that pushed the limits of physics, and perhaps even reality itself.

But what did *Die Glocke* look like? How did it allegedly function? What clues exist, and where do the blueprints—if any—come from? In this chapter, we reconstruct the puzzle of the Bell's alleged technology using accounts from military researchers, postwar testimony, speculative physics, and investigative journalism.

1. Physical Description: The Bell-Shaped Mystery

The name *Die Glocke* derives from its physical form: a **bell-shaped metallic structure**, reportedly:

- **Height:** Approx. 2.7 meters (9 feet)
- **Diameter at base:** Approx. 1.5 meters (5 feet)
- **Outer shell:** Likely composed of **heavy-duty, lead-lined metal**, possibly cladded in **ceramic** or **beryllium oxide** to contain radiation or electromagnetic discharge
- **Surface features:** Smooth, possibly engraved or fitted with protruding nodes or insulation rivets

This form was described in postwar interviews and detailed most extensively in Igor Witkowski's *The Truth About the Wunderwaffe* (2003), based on intelligence transcripts he claimed to have accessed from Polish archives. Eyewitnesses likened the device to a **large industrial container** or **casing for a turbine**, yet with no identifiable external power source or exhaust system.

Sources:

- Witkowski, I. (2003). *The Truth About the Wunderwaffe*
- Farrell, J. P. (2004). *Reich of the Black Sun*

---

2. Internal Components: Counter-Rotation and Xerum 525

The most crucial aspect of the Bell's alleged functionality was the presence of two **counter-rotating cylinders** within the casing. These were designed to spin at high speeds—possibly tens of thousands of revolutions per minute—in opposite directions.

Purpose of Rotation

According to theorists, this internal counter-rotation:

- Generated **intense torsion fields** (linked to unverified theories of scalar physics or torsion physics)
- Created a **vacuum plasma field** or electromagnetic vortex
- Was responsible for manipulating gravity or localized spacetime

Xerum 525

Contained inside the rotating drums was a highly mysterious and hazardous substance known as **"Xerum 525."**

- **Described as:** A violet, mercury-like fluid, stored in lead cylinders approx. 1 meter long and encased in a heavy metal
- **Highly radioactive and toxic**
- Possibly a **radioisotope of mercury, red mercury,** or some form of **plasma reactant**

No known isotope matches the description exactly, though theorists speculate it could have been a synthesized **isomer or metastable nuclear fuel**.

Sources:

- Witkowski, I. (2003). *The Truth About the Wunderwaffe*
- Marrs, J. (2008). *The Rise of the Fourth Reich*
- Cook, N. (2001). *The Hunt for Zero Point*

---

3. Alleged Principles of Operation

The most controversial and extraordinary claim about *Die Glocke* is that it produced effects **unexplainable by standard physics**. Theorized principles of operation vary widely depending on the interpretation, but several consistent themes emerge:

A. Torsion Field Theory

- Rooted in suppressed Soviet-era research, torsion fields are hypothesized as a fifth fundamental force.
- Created by the interaction of **spinning, high-density materials**, particularly under electromagnetic excitation.
- Believed to affect gravity, time, and even biological systems.

Researchers like **Dr. Nikolai Kozyrev** and **Gennady Shipov** (working decades later) developed models for torsion fields that some claim mirror the Bell's alleged operation.

B. Zero-Point Energy (ZPE) Extraction

- The Bell might have been an attempt to **extract usable energy from the quantum vacuum**.
- Counter-rotation and high voltages could disrupt the quantum field and extract **virtual particles**.

C. Anti-Gravity and Field Propulsion

- *Die Glocke* may have created a localized **gravitational distortion**, allowing levitation or inertial dampening.

- Some link this to postwar **UFO propulsion systems**, implying a technological lineage.

Sources:

- Kozyrev, N. A. (1950s-60s). Time and Torsion Research
- Farrell, J. P. (2004). *Reich of the Black Sun*
- LaViolette, P. A. (2008). *Secrets of Antigravity Propulsion*

---

4. The Bell's Platform: The Henge Structure

The massive concrete structure known as **"The Henge"** near the Wenceslas Mine in Lower Silesia is believed by some to have been a **test rig** or **support platform** for *Die Glocke*.

Characteristics:

- 12 large concrete pillars in a circular pattern, approx. 10 meters in diameter
- No pipework, cooling tanks, or smoke ducts present—suggesting non-industrial use
- Reinforced concrete with potential electrical conduits or mount points on top

Some theorists suggest this acted as a **magnetic stabilizing cradle**, allowing the Bell to **levitate** within the ring during tests. Others posit it was meant to **anchor** the device against high internal forces or torsional backlash during operation.

Skeptics argue it is a remnant of an **industrial cooling tower**, though no standard schematic has matched it conclusively.

Sources:

- Site surveys from Ludwikowice Kłodzkie, Poland
- Witkowski, I. (2003)
- Polish Ministry of Culture, Owl Mountains Archives (public archaeology notes)

5. Power and Containment Systems

While no photographs or blueprints of *Die Glocke* have surfaced, descriptions imply it required **massive electrical input**:

- Possibly fed by a **dedicated power station or transformer bank**
- Cables and generators reportedly found around the mine site postwar
- Operation likely demanded **cooling systems** to dissipate heat and EM buildup

Containment systems were rumored to include:

- **Radiation shielding** made from lead and high-density ceramics
- **Faraday cages** to suppress EM leakage
- Underground **blast chambers** for test safety

Local accounts report **blue and violet flashes**, low-frequency pulses, and sudden deaths among test personnel, suggesting possible **electromagnetic or neutron radiation** exposure.

---

6. Comparative Analysis: Modern and Theoretical Parallels

Despite lacking solid proof, elements of *Die Glocke*'s alleged technology echo postwar advances:

A. Electrogravitics and Biefeld-Brown Effect

- Postwar research into **electrokinetic propulsion** mirrors Bell-like systems
- Claims that high-voltage capacitors could produce lift or inertial cancellation

B. Classified U.S. Programs

- Projects such as **Project Winterhaven** and **GRASP** explored gravity research during and after Operation Paperclip
- Reverse engineering of Nazi technology hinted at in U.S. Air Force archives

C. The ARV (Alien Reproduction Vehicle)

- Described by whistleblowers like **Mark McCandlish**, the ARV (a.k.a. "Flux Liner") shares the Bell's profile: **rotating fields, plasma toroids**, and **gravitational lensing**

Sources:

- McCandlish, M. (Disclosure Project testimony, 2001)
- LaViolette, P. A. (2008)
- U.S. Air Force Research Laboratory (AFRL) papers on advanced propulsion (declassified segments)

No known blueprints, prototypes, or scientific logs of *Die Glocke* have ever been found. Its engineering remains a matter of speculation—pieced together from witness testimony, circumstantial evidence, and theoretical extrapolation.

Yet the consistency of descriptions, the overlap with experimental propulsion concepts, and the strange ruins in Silesia form a narrative that is hard to ignore. Whether the Bell was an early prototype of **exotic propulsion**, a **radioactive hoax**, or something **even stranger**, its technological legend continues to inspire and provoke.

The question remains: if *Die Glocke* was just myth, **why did it leave such a clear technological silhouette** in our imaginations—and perhaps, in our skies?

Suggested References and Further Reading

1. Igor Witkowski – *The Truth About the Wunderwaffe* (2003)
2. Joseph P. Farrell – *Reich of the Black Sun* (2004), *The SS Brotherhood of the Bell* (2006)
3. Nick Cook – *The Hunt for Zero Point* (2001)
4. Paul A. LaViolette – *Secrets of Antigravity Propulsion* (2008)
5. Jim Marrs – *The Rise of the Fourth Reich* (2008)

6. Declassified U.S. Air Force and CIA technical memos (1950s–70s)
7. McCandlish, M. – Disclosure testimony (2001)

Chapter 7: The Chrononaut Theories – Time Travel Claims and Temporal Experiments

"When dealing with Die Glocke, one must be prepared to cross the frontier not only of science—but of time itself."
— Joseph P. Farrell, *The SS Brotherhood of the Bell* (2006)

Introduction: Bending the Arrow of Time

Among the most extraordinary claims surrounding *Die Glocke* is that the device was not just a propulsion experiment—but a **temporal machine**: a device that allegedly manipulated the flow of time, opened rifts in space-time, or generated closed time-like curves. These claims, though often dismissed by mainstream historians, persist in both fringe physics and black project circles.

This chapter explores what has come to be known as the **Chrononaut Theories**—the belief that Die Glocke's experiments under SS General Hans Kammler were intended not only to break the laws of motion but to **puncture the fabric of time**.

1. Origins of the Time Travel Claims

The time travel narrative first gained traction through the work of Polish journalist and researcher **Igor Witkowski**, whose interviews with an unnamed Polish intelligence source provided descriptions of early German research into **temporal displacement** using Die Glocke. In his landmark work *The Truth About the Wunderwaffe* (2003), Witkowski recounts a series of classified interrogation transcripts, allegedly conducted by Allied forces after the war.

According to these reports:

- Several scientists working on the Bell died or became mentally unstable following tests.
- Witnesses described visual anomalies such as **"freezing air"**, **"distorted light"**, and **"blurring of objects."**
- Objects placed near the Bell during activation would sometimes **decay rapidly** or **vanish**.

These phenomena, interpreted through a modern lens, resemble side effects associated with **strong gravitational or temporal field distortions**, such as predicted by general relativity.

Primary Source:

- Witkowski, Igor. *The Truth About the Wunderwaffe*. European History Press, 2003.

---

2. Theoretical Basis: Temporal Physics and Relativity

While mainstream physics does not support time travel as depicted in fiction, **Einstein's theory of general relativity** allows for temporal manipulation under specific extreme conditions.

A. Closed Time-Like Curves (CTCs)

CTCs are solutions to Einstein's field equations that loop back in time. These could theoretically occur under conditions such as:

- **Rotating black holes** (Kerr metrics)
- **Tipler cylinders** (hypothetical, infinitely long rotating structures)
- **Intense gravitational torsion fields**, potentially like those theorized around Die Glocke

B. Gravitational Time Dilation

A proven aspect of general relativity where time passes differently in strong gravitational fields. If the Bell created localized fields of sufficient intensity, objects or observers nearby could **experience time differently**.

C. Torsion Fields

Torsion-based physics—pursued in the Soviet Union by **Kozyrev, Shipov**, and others—suggests that rotating massive objects can twist spacetime, possibly enabling information or particles to move backward in time.

These theories, though speculative, are consistent with what the Bell was allegedly doing: using **counter-rotating drums**, **high-voltage discharges**, and **exotic materials** to distort spacetime.

Key Theoretical References:

- Einstein, A. (1915). General Relativity Field Equations
- Gödel, K. (1949). "Example of a new type of cosmological solutions of Einstein's field equations"
- Kozyrev, Nikolai A. (1950s–70s). *Torsion Field Studies*

---

3. Alleged Experiments and Effects

Accounts from Witkowski and others describe several Bell tests that resulted in **anomalous temporal phenomena**.

A. Accelerated Decay and Aging

Test subjects (plants, animals) placed near the Bell allegedly:

- Aged rapidly within minutes
- Crystallized or liquified internally
- Showed tissue necrosis inconsistent with radiation or chemical exposure

This has been interpreted as **biological time distortion**, possibly from localized relativistic fields or electromagnetic pulse effects disrupting biological rhythms.

B. Vanishing Objects

Reports state that **metallic or ceramic objects placed near the Bell** would:

- Blink out of existence
- Reappear with physical alterations

- Be "phased" partially into the test platform or floor

This could suggest **displacement across space and/or time**, or the breakdown of local atomic cohesion due to quantum effects.

C. Human Exposure and Madness

Several scientists were reportedly institutionalized after Bell tests. One claimed to have **"seen into the past"** during activation. Others experienced:

- Temporal disorientation
- Auditory hallucinations of "voices from nowhere"
- Dissociation and memory loss

Such symptoms may be explained by **high EMF exposure**, but believers claim it indicates **brief temporal dislocation or quantum consciousness anomalies**.

---

4. Kammler's Secret Agenda: Chrono-Weapons?

SS General Hans Kammler—already in charge of advanced rocket and jet programs—was allegedly fixated on **non-conventional breakthroughs** that could win the war in a single strike. If true, the possibility of time manipulation would have been the **ultimate strategic weapon**.

Possible Kammler Objectives:

- **Send information or technology back in time**
- **Create temporal stasis for weapons or personnel**
- **View or manipulate past or future battle conditions**
- **Escape** Nazi defeat by sending key personnel forward or backward in time

A few speculative accounts claim Kammler himself **vanished mysteriously** in 1945—possibly with the Bell. One theory even suggests a **"temporal exfiltration"**, though this remains pure speculation.

Sources:

- Farrell, J. P. *The SS Brotherhood of the Bell.* 2006.

- Marrs, Jim. *The Rise of the Fourth Reich*. 2008.
- U.S. Army G-2 Archives (declassified), fragmentary references to "Chronos device"

5. Postwar Echoes: Operation Paperclip and Missing Time

After the war, many German scientists, including those linked to Kammler's circle, were absorbed into **Operation Paperclip** in the U.S. One of the more mysterious aspects of this program was the absence of records for certain personnel believed to have worked on *Die Glocke*.

Meanwhile, in the U.S., the **Philadelphia Experiment** (1943) and later **Montauk Project** (1980s) featured strikingly similar themes:

- Time displacement
- Spacetime "bubble" effects
- Biological degradation of test subjects

Some theorists believe these projects represent **continuations of Nazi chrono-research** under new management, using ideas harvested from *Die Glocke* and related experiments.

Notable Parallels:

- "Project Montauk" – Claims of time tunnels and mind control
- "Project Pegasus" – Testimonies by Andrew Basiago alleging time travel technologies derived from Nazi research
- *Majestic-12* documents – Indirect reference to "temporal engines" used in exotic craft

6. Critical Perspectives and Scientific Skepticism

Many physicists and historians reject the Chrononaut Theories as **pseudoscientific mythology**, pointing to:

- Lack of direct evidence: No blueprints, physical remnants, or verified eyewitnesses.

- Absence of test logs: All alleged data comes from secondhand accounts or unverified sources.
- Misinterpretation of scientific concepts: Torsion fields and CTCs are unverified and largely theoretical.

Nevertheless, the **persistence of the narrative**, its alignment with certain declassified research threads, and its integration into U.S. postwar research keep the theory alive.

Even if the Bell did not cause time travel, it **provoked the imagination** of generations of researchers who saw in it not just a machine—but a symbol of **humanity's dangerous reach beyond its grasp**.

Was Die Glocke a time machine? Perhaps not in the literal sense. But something about the device—its secrecy, effects, and legacy—echoes with the sense that **time itself was disturbed** by its presence.

Whether a technological relic, a metaphysical experiment, or a myth woven from fear and ambition, the Chrononaut Theories endure as part of the strange gravitational field that surrounds *Die Glocke*. Even now, the Bell seems to pull us—not just toward the past—but toward **what might have been**.

Suggested References and Further Reading

1. Igor Witkowski – *The Truth About the Wunderwaffe* (2003)
2. Joseph P. Farrell – *The SS Brotherhood of the Bell* (2006)
3. Nick Cook – *The Hunt for Zero Point* (2001)
4. Jim Marrs – *The Rise of the Fourth Reich* (2008)
5. Kurt Gödel – "Time Travel in Relativity" (1949)
6. Nikolai Kozyrev – *The Causal Mechanics of Time* (1958)
7. CIA FOIA Docs – "Electrogravitics and Temporal Anomalies" (declassified 1990s)

8. Andrew Basiago – Montauk and Project Pegasus Interviews (2004–2012)

Chapter 8: Anti-Gravity and the Vril Drive – Connections to Exotic Propulsion and Energy

"What if the legends of the Vril Society weren't myth, but fragments of a classified technological reality—one that harnessed the very fabric of space itself?"
— Joseph P. Farrell, *Reich of the Black Sun* (2004)

Introduction: From Myth to Mechanism

Of all the claims surrounding *Die Glocke*, none is more provocative—or more speculative—than its alleged connection to **anti-gravity propulsion**. At the heart of this theory lies a nexus of wartime black projects, obscure German esoteric societies, and physics far ahead of its time. According to researchers and independent theorists, the Bell was more than an experiment in energy or time—it was a prototype for a **Vril-powered flight engine**, capable of lifting itself free from Earth's gravitational field.

This chapter explores the alleged relationship between *Die Glocke*, exotic propulsion, and the so-called **Vril Drive**—a term associated with secret Nazi engineering projects based on advanced physics, torsion fields, and zero-point energy. While the evidence remains circumstantial, the conceptual parallels with later developments in aerospace and electrogravitics are hard to ignore.

1. The Concept of Vril: From Fiction to Fascination

The term **"Vril"** originates from the 1871 novel *The Coming Race* by British author Edward Bulwer-Lytton. In this work, an underground race of beings known as the **Vril-ya** wielded an all-powerful energy source called "Vril" that enabled levitation, telepathy, and destructive force.

Despite its fictional origin, Vril became a central theme in esoteric circles, particularly in pre-Nazi Germany. By the 1920s and 30s, several fringe groups—including the **Vril Society** and the **Thule Society**—were rumored to be exploring ways to tap into this **"cosmic life force"**, often mixing mysticism with pseudo-scientific theories.

Vril in Occult-Scientific Thought

- **Seen as aetheric or zero-point energy**—a limitless field from which energy and propulsion could be drawn.
- Tied to ancient Atlantean myths, Aryan racial ideology, and the belief in a lost technology that predated human civilization.
- Became, in Nazi fringe science, a **symbol for untapped, non-electrical, field-based energy**.

References:

- Bulwer-Lytton, Edward. *The Coming Race* (1871)
- Goodrick-Clarke, Nicholas. *The Occult Roots of Nazism* (1992)

---

2. Nazi Interest in Exotic Propulsion

While the Vril Society's actual existence is debated, the Nazi regime's interest in **alternative propulsion and breakthrough physics** is well documented. Between 1940 and 1945, the SS, under General Hans Kammler, established a parallel research empire focusing on **unconventional energy and flight systems**.

Key indicators of this interest:

- Projects housed under the **SS Entwicklungsstelle IV** (Kammler's R&D department).
- Construction of deep underground labs and high-voltage facilities at sites like **Wenceslas Mine** and **Project Riese**.
- Eyewitness accounts and postwar interrogations referencing **rotating field generators, liquid metals**, and "levitation" experiments.

The infamous *Die Glocke*—a bell-shaped, rotating device—fits these experimental profiles, with its core feature being a **dual counter-rotating** chamber filled with a mysterious substance called **Xerum 525**, designed to generate powerful magnetic and gravitational anomalies.

3. The Bell as a Vril Propulsion Engine

According to **Igor Witkowski** and **Joseph P. Farrell**, the operational mechanics of *Die Glocke* resemble what modern theorists call **torsion-based or electrogravitic propulsion**:

Alleged Working Principles:

- **Counter-rotating magnetic fields** generate intense space-time torsion.
- Interaction with **Xerum 525** (possibly a mercury-based isotope in a plasma state) creates an internal pressure differential or field bubble.
- The result is a **mass-reduction or gravity-alteration effect**, potentially lifting the device.

Some reports suggest the Bell glowed with **violet or blue light**, emitted a **high-frequency hum**, and had devastating effects on biological tissues—consistent with **high-energy electromagnetic or torsion field emissions**.

If accurate, these properties align closely with **electrogravitic theories** proposed decades later by researchers like **Thomas Townsend Brown** and **Podkletnov**, suggesting that Nazi Germany may have been testing **field propulsion** ahead of its time.

4. Die Glocke and the "Repulsine" Connection

Another piece of the puzzle comes from Austrian engineer **Viktor Schauberger**, who worked on implosion-based flight craft for the Third Reich. Schauberger's prototypes, especially the **Repulsine A and B**, used **vortex physics** and rotating disks to manipulate lift and thrust.

Shared Design Concepts:

- **Rotation-driven propulsion**
- **Non-combustion-based energy source**

- Emphasis on natural energy harmonics and vacuum flow

Schauberger's writings repeatedly refer to energy as *"implosion-based,"* the opposite of explosive combustion. After the war, he was taken to the U.S. under duress, where his concepts were quietly studied by intelligence agencies.

Although Schauberger was not directly linked to the Bell project, the technological parallels—and the shared involvement of Kammler's SS programs—suggest potential overlap or knowledge transfer.

References:

- Alexandersson, Olof. *Living Water: Viktor Schauberger and the Secrets of Natural Energy* (1990)
- Callum Coats. *The Energy Evolution: Harnessing Free Energy from Nature* (2001)

---

5. Zero-Point Energy and Exotic Field Drives

The alleged anti-gravity function of Die Glocke also aligns with emerging concepts of **zero-point energy (ZPE)**, the theoretical baseline energy present in all space.

Properties of ZPE:

- Exists in a vacuum, even at absolute zero
- Proposed as a source of **reactionless propulsion**
- Explored by researchers like **Harold Puthoff, Halton Arp**, and **John Hutchison**

In this model, *Die Glocke* may have been a **field resonator**—exciting the vacuum energy of space and creating a lifting force. The **Vril Drive**, then, would be a wartime term for a ZPE-based gravity engine.

Several U.S. aerospace companies, including **Lockheed Martin's Skunk Works**, have since shown interest in ZPE and field propulsion—leading some theorists to speculate that Nazi discoveries were absorbed postwar via **Operation Paperclip**.

References:

- Puthoff, Harold E. "Gravity as a Zero-Point Fluctuation Force." Physical Review A, 1989.
- Farrell, Joseph P. *Reich of the Black Sun* (2004)

---

6. Postwar Legacy: From Bell to UFOs?

In the decades following World War II, reports of **disk-shaped craft, field-propelled objects**, and **black triangles** surged across the U.S. and Europe. While often attributed to extraterrestrials, some theorists argue these sightings may stem from **Nazi-derived propulsion systems** perfected in secret programs.

Supporting Clues:

- Reports of "Nazi flying saucers" in South America (Base 211, Antarctica)
- Witness accounts of recovered Bell-like technology in postwar Germany
- Persistent U.S. military interest in **electrogravitic** and **non-Newtonian propulsion**

Projects like **TR-3B, Aurora**, and **Project Silverbug** all featured propulsion concepts analogous to what the Bell was alleged to do—using **field manipulation** rather than jet or rocket thrust.

Further Reading:

- Nick Cook. *The Hunt for Zero Point* (2001)
- Timothy Good. *Above Top Secret* (1987)

Whether the Bell ever achieved anti-gravity flight remains uncertain. But the converging lines of evidence—ranging from SS black projects and esoteric societies to postwar military experiments—suggest that *Die Glocke* may have been the **nexus of an exotic propulsion paradigm** that never entered public view.

The Vril Drive, as a concept, may be less about a specific engine and more about an **alternative vision of technology**—one rooted not in combustion and force, but in **harmony with fields, resonance, and the quantum vacuum**.

If the Nazis did make contact with this force, they may not have fully understood what they had. But the legacy of Die Glocke and the Vril Drive continues to reverberate—through myths, conspiracies, and perhaps even through the skies.

Suggested References and Further Reading

1. Igor Witkowski – *The Truth About the Wunderwaffe* (2003)
2. Joseph P. Farrell – *Reich of the Black Sun* (2004), *SS Brotherhood of the Bell* (2006)
3. Olof Alexandersson – *Living Water: Viktor Schauberger and the Secrets of Natural Energy* (1990)
4. Nick Cook – *The Hunt for Zero Point* (2001)
5. Harold E. Puthoff – "Gravity as a Zero-Point Fluctuation Force" (1989)
6. Nicholas Goodrick-Clarke – *The Occult Roots of Nazism* (1992)
7. Declassified FOIA Documents – U.S. research into electrogravitics (1950s–2000s)

Chapter 9: The Liquid Code – "Xerum 525" and the Alchemy of the Bell

---

"Xerum 525 was said to glow, to kill within minutes, and to be the heart of the Bell. But what was it—an isotope, an alchemical compound, or something entirely outside our science?"

Introduction: A Liquid Wrapped in Mystery

Amid the cryptic references to *Die Glocke*, no detail is as simultaneously specific and elusive as **Xerum 525**—a code name whispered in declassified reports, conspiracy literature, and wartime testimonies. Described as a **dense, violet-reddish metallic liquid** stored in flask-like containers, this substance was reportedly crucial to the operation of the Bell device, powering its rotating magnetic chambers and producing strange biological and gravitational effects.

Despite its sinister beauty and alleged lethality, no known compound in modern science perfectly matches the characteristics attributed to Xerum 525. Its mystique has led researchers to link it to **red mercury, radioactive isotopes, plasma-state fuels**, and even **esoteric alchemical substances**.

In this chapter, we examine everything we know—and theorize—about Xerum 525: its physical properties, possible origins, theoretical mechanisms, and its place at the very core of the Nazi Bell mystery.

1. Descriptions from Witkowski and Beyond

The primary source of the Xerum 525 narrative comes from Polish journalist and military historian **Igor Witkowski,** whose 2000 book *Prawda o Wunderwaffe* (*The Truth About the Wunderwaffe*) first introduced the concept based on alleged interrogation transcripts of **SS officer Jakob Sporrenberg**.

According to Witkowski:

- Xerum 525 was a **heavy, reddish metallic liquid** with a consistency similar to **mercury**, but far denser.
- It was **housed in lead-lined, foot-long containers** encased in ceramic insulation.
- It was **highly radioactive and lethal**—exposure killed test subjects and animals in proximity during early experiments.
- It was used inside the **counter-rotating drum chambers of the Bell**, possibly in a vortex or high-energy plasma state.

Quote from Witkowski:

"It was almost certainly radioactive... it may have been a compound of mercury with thorium or another heavy element, possibly in a colloidal suspension."

References:

- Igor Witkowski, *The Truth About the Wunderwaffe* (2003, English edition)

2. Red Mercury: A Modern Myth or a Nuclear Reality?

The characteristics of Xerum 525 closely resemble another shadowy substance: **Red Mercury**.

Red Mercury Allegations:

- Appeared in intelligence reports during the Cold War as a **dense, red-hued mercury compound**.
- Rumored to be used as a **nuclear fusion catalyst** or **stealth explosive material**.
- Reports claimed it was **superconductive, anti-radar**, or could create **gravitational anomalies**.
- Never publicly verified, but black-market samples circulated in the 1980s–1990s.

Some theorists believe **Red Mercury and Xerum 525 are the same**—or at least represent the same family of high-energy, mercury-based substances used for exotic or quantum applications.

In both cases, the implications point to **non-conventional physics**: field manipulation, quantum resonance, or even **mass-altering properties** when under rotation or EM stimulation.

References:

- BBC News, "The Red Mercury Hoax" (1999)
- Joseph P. Farrell, *SS Brotherhood of the Bell* (2006)

3. Nuclear Possibilities: Mercury Isotopes and Heavy Elements

Could Xerum 525 have been a **real compound**, derived from nuclear or chemical experimentation?

Theories include:

- **Mercury-Thorium Plasma:** A mix of volatile mercury with thorium-232, which is weakly radioactive and capable of neutron absorption under specific conditions.
- **Mercury-Antimony Oxides:** Used in certain priming explosives—stable, but highly reactive under EM induction.
- **Mercury-204 or 196:** Isotopes with potential (theoretical) use in **low-yield fusion or neutron capture technologies**.

Mercury is especially interesting in this context because of its **diamagnetic properties**, which allow it to resist magnetic fields. When spun at high speeds and subjected to electric charge, **liquid mercury can generate unusual field effects**, a principle some believe could be exploited in **magnetogravitic propulsion**.

---

4. Torsion Field Fuel? Esoteric Physics Perspectives

Some researchers working in alternative physics believe Xerum 525 was **not chemically exotic** so much as it was **energetically tuned**—possibly functioning as a **torsion field medium** or a **non-linear dielectric fluid**.

Torsion Theories (Kozyrev, Akimov):

- Torsion fields are theoretical distortions in spacetime caused by spinning masses.
- A high-density, coherent fluid (like mercury) could hypothetically act as an amplifier or vector for these fields.
- Under high-frequency EM rotation, the medium could alter **inertial mass**, **time flow**, or **gravitational coupling**.

The alleged lethality of Xerum 525 to organic tissue could result from **unshielded scalar/torsion emissions**, which would disrupt cellular processes even without ionizing radiation.

References:

- Nikolai Kozyrev, "Causal Mechanics and the Active Properties of Time" (1958)
- Gennady Shipov, *A Theory of Physical Vacuum* (1993)

5. Alchemical Echoes: The Philosopher's Mercury

Curiously, the descriptions of Xerum 525 echo the medieval concept of the **"Philosopher's Mercury"**—an essential ingredient in alchemical transformation.

- Known as **"Mercurius"**, this mystical fluid was said to be the **soul of all metals** and key to achieving transmutation.
- Alchemists described it as volatile, glowing, capable of **transcending matter**, and both deadly and divine.

Heinrich Himmler's SS, heavily influenced by **esoteric and Hermetic thought**, may have seen no contradiction in blending **particle physics** with **alchemical mysticism**. The search for a **red liquid of transformation**—capable of converting mass, time, or even life—was arguably the perfect metaphor for Nazi ambitions.

6. Practical Use in the Bell Mechanism

What was Xerum 525 actually doing inside *Die Glocke*?

According to reconstructions:

- It was **rotated at extremely high RPMs** inside two counter-rotating drums, creating intense centrifugal and EM fields.
- Subjected to **electrostatic pulsing or oscillation**, possibly creating **standing waves** in the containment chamber.
- Functioned either as an **energy plasma, dielectric medium**, or **reaction mass** for field generation.

The result was an experimental condition in which **mass was manipulated, biological effects occurred**, and possibly **temporal shifts** were observed (as claimed by some witnesses and later theorists).

Whether fact or fiction, this concept matches **later propulsion research**, including:

- **Brown–Biefeld Effect**

- **Podkletnov Gravity Shielding**
- **NASA's EM Drive and Q-Thruster concepts**

---

7. Disappearance and Legacy

After 1945, no verifiable samples or documents regarding Xerum 525 have surfaced. It is speculated that:

- All samples were **destroyed or captured** by Soviet or American forces.
- The substance was **rediscovered** under new names in Cold War black projects.
- It never existed in a physical sense, but was a **code name** for a physics condition or principle.

Nonetheless, the legend of Xerum 525 lives on—in red mercury scares, fringe propulsion theories, and the persistent belief that **somewhere, someone cracked the code** of gravity itself.

The story of Xerum 525 reminds us how blurred the lines become between **science**, **myth**, and **military secrecy**. Whether a real substance, a misunderstood technology, or a deliberate disinformation tactic, Xerum 525 remains one of the most tantalizing clues in the *Die Glocke* saga.

It was the liquid at the heart of the Bell—lethal, luminous, and entirely unknown.

Suggested References and Further Reading

1. Igor Witkowski – *The Truth About the Wunderwaffe* (2003)
2. Joseph P. Farrell – *SS Brotherhood of the Bell* (2006)
3. BBC News – "The Red Mercury Hoax" (1999)
4. Gennady Shipov – *The Theory of Physical Vacuum* (1993)
5. Nick Cook – *The Hunt for Zero Point* (2001)

6. Edward Bulwer-Lytton – *The Coming Race* (1871)
7. William Lyne – *Occult Ether Physics* (1997)

Chapter 10: The Bell and the Brain – Experiments on Biological Effects, Rumors of Death and Mutation

"Exposure to the Bell was said to cause immediate disorientation, neurological damage, and fatal radiation sickness—a curse whispered among the few who glimpsed its deadly glow."
— Joseph P. Farrell, *SS Brotherhood of the Bell* (2006)

Introduction: The Deadly Heart of Die Glocke

While much of the *Die Glocke* mystery centers on physics, propulsion, and esoteric science, a darker, more human story lies beneath the layers of secrecy: the alleged **biological effects** of the Bell's operation. Eyewitness testimonies, declassified interrogation reports, and postwar investigations reveal that *Die Glocke* was not merely a mechanical experiment but a potentially lethal source of **radiation, toxicity,** and **neurological disruption**.

This chapter investigates the claims that exposure to the Bell's emissions caused **instant death, mental breakdowns,** and **mutations** in test animals and possibly humans. It delves into how these effects influenced Nazi research protocols and the ultimate fate of the Bell's test subjects.

1. Reports from the Wenceslas Site: Immediate Effects

Accounts from the underground testing facility at the **Wenceslas Mine** (Lower Silesia) describe chilling scenes:

- Workers near the Bell heard a **high-pitched humming or whining**, sometimes compared to a **tuning fork at unbearable frequencies**.

- Animals exposed to the Bell's operation—rabbits, dogs, and monkeys—were reported to **suffer neurological convulsions** and often died within minutes or hours.
- Personnel without protective gear developed **severe headaches, nausea, and hallucinations**.
- Some witnesses described **strange neurological symptoms**: loss of balance, memory lapses, and uncontrollable tremors.

These symptoms are consistent with exposure to **intense electromagnetic radiation**, **ionizing radiation**, or exotic fields that interfere with brain function.

References:

- Witkowski, Igor. *The Truth About the Wunderwaffe* (2003)
- Anonymous testimonies in declassified German archives (circa 1945)

2. The Lethality of Xerum 525

Central to the Bell's biological dangers was **Xerum 525**, the mysterious red mercury-like fluid at its core (see Chapter 9). Experiments showed that:

- Xerum 525 emitted **radioactive or torsion field emissions** lethal to living cells.
- Test animals placed near containers of Xerum 525 developed **internal bleeding, cellular breakdown**, and **organ failure**.
- Prolonged exposure reportedly caused **mutation in DNA**, though these claims are anecdotal and lack scientific verification.

The combination of **toxic chemical properties** and **unusual energetic emissions** made Xerum 525 a lethal hazard, complicating experimentation.

3. Human Test Subjects: The Grim Reality

Though concrete evidence is scarce, various sources hint that human volunteers or prisoners—possibly from concentration camps—were exposed to the Bell's effects as part of experimental protocols.

- SS officers and scientists allegedly observed **rapid-onset radiation sickness**.
- Some subjects reportedly suffered **acute brain hemorrhaging** and **psychotic episodes** shortly after exposure.
- A handful of documents mention **neurological testing**, possibly attempting to map the brain's reaction to torsion or electromagnetic fields.

Such experiments, if true, reflect the Nazi regime's infamous willingness to sacrifice human life in pursuit of technological breakthroughs.

References:

- Joseph P. Farrell, *SS Brotherhood of the Bell* (2006)
- Testimony transcripts from postwar war crimes investigations

---

4. Mutation and Evolution: Fact or Fear?

More speculative—but widely circulated—are reports that the Bell's radiation induced **mutations** in living organisms:

- Some accounts claim animals developed **extra limbs**, **neural deformities**, or **accelerated aging**.
- Alleged survivors of exposure were rumored to exhibit **heightened sensory perception** or **psychic abilities**.
- These stories echo Nazi ambitions in **racial engineering** and **biological enhancement**.

While lacking scientific rigor, these rumors contribute to the mythos of *Die Glocke* as a tool not just for physics but for biological transformation.

---

5. The Bell's Brainwave Interference: Neuro-Field Hypothesis

Modern theories propose that the Bell generated complex **electromagnetic or scalar fields** that interfered directly with brainwave patterns:

- Operating frequencies may have disrupted **alpha, beta, and gamma waves**, causing disorientation or hallucinations.
- Some speculate the Bell's fields could affect **neural coherence**, potentially explaining reported mental disturbances or deaths.
- The "brainwave interference" hypothesis aligns with experimental research into **electromagnetic hypersensitivity** and **neurological effects of pulsed fields**.

This line of thought has prompted comparisons with modern military experiments in **non-lethal mind control** and **psychotronic warfare**.

References:

- Michael Persinger, "The Neuropsychological Effects of Electromagnetic Fields," *Perceptual and Motor Skills* (1996)
- Joseph P. Farrell, *SS Brotherhood of the Bell* (2006)

---

6. Safety Protocols and the Bell's Operational Limits

The documented dangers led to strict operational rules:

- Test personnel were required to wear protective gear, including lead-lined suits and respirators.
- Exposure times were limited to seconds or minutes.
- Remote operation was favored whenever possible, with many experiments conducted underground or behind shielding.

Despite these precautions, accidents and fatalities reportedly occurred regularly, contributing to the Bell's eventual abandonment.

---

7. Legacy of Biological Horror

The Bell's biological impact serves as a grim reminder that cutting-edge technology can bear a heavy human cost. Its toxic energy disrupted not only physical matter but the essence of life—brain, cells, and DNA.

This intersection of **physics and biology** anticipates modern concerns about **electromagnetic pollution, radiation safety,** and the ethical limits of experimentation.

Die Glocke was not just a machine of science or myth—it was a **biological weapon of sorts**, an experiment in the terrifying power of exotic fields on living organisms. Its lethal emissions silenced many witnesses, and its biological horrors remain part of the shadowy legacy of Nazi secret weapons.

Whether as a cautionary tale or a dark beacon in the search for advanced propulsion, the Bell's effects on brain and body remain one of its most haunting mysteries.

Suggested References and Further Reading

1. Igor Witkowski – *The Truth About the Wunderwaffe* (2003)
2. Joseph P. Farrell – *SS Brotherhood of the Bell* (2006)
3. Michael Persinger – "The Neuropsychological Effects of Electromagnetic Fields," *Perceptual and Motor Skills* (1996)
4. Declassified German and Allied interrogation transcripts (1945–1947)
5. Nicholas Goodrick-Clarke – *The Occult Roots of Nazism* (1992)

Part III: War and Disappearance

Chapter 11: The Fall of Berlin, The Rise of Secrets – Nazi Desperation in the Final Days of the War

---

"As the Red Army closed in, the Nazi regime's obsession with Wunderwaffe became a fevered race against time — a desperate hope that secret weapons might turn defeat into victory."
— Nikolaus von Below, *Hitler's Last Days* (1958)

Introduction: The Twilight of the Third Reich

By early 1945, Nazi Germany was crumbling on every front. The Allied forces had breached the Western borders, and the Soviet Red Army was sweeping through Eastern Europe, closing in on Berlin itself. The war was lost, and the Reich's leadership faced the grim reality of total defeat.

In these final, chaotic months, the Nazis intensified their focus on **Wunderwaffe**—"wonder weapons"—hoping to reverse their fortunes with last-ditch technological marvels, including the elusive *Die Glocke*. This chapter explores how desperation shaped Nazi actions, influenced secret weapons programs, and sowed the seeds for the postwar myths and conspiracies surrounding hidden Nazi technology.

---

1. Berlin Besieged: Strategic Collapse and Psychological Turmoil

The Battle of Berlin (April–May 1945) was a brutal final stand. Despite overwhelming Soviet superiority, Hitler insisted on holding the city to the last man.

- **Morale was shattered** among soldiers and civilians; rumors of secret weapons fueled both hope and hysteria.
- The Nazi command structure became fragmented, with power struggles and chaotic communications.

- Many scientists and engineers associated with secret projects, including those tied to *Die Glocke*, were evacuated or hidden to avoid capture.

2. Kammler's Role: The SS General's Last Orders

SS General **Hans Kammler**, allegedly in charge of many top-secret weapons projects, including the Bell, was a pivotal figure in these last days.

- Kammler was tasked with **safeguarding advanced technology** and personnel from Soviet capture.
- He reportedly issued orders to **destroy documents**, **relocate equipment**, and **erase traces** of forbidden research.
- Kammler's fate after the war remains unclear—some say he died, others claim he escaped with secret knowledge.

His role symbolizes the Nazi regime's frantic efforts to **salvage its scientific legacy** even as the Reich itself fell apart.

3. Evacuation of Secret Projects

The Nazi leadership orchestrated massive evacuations:

- Facilities such as the **Wenceslas Mine**, where *Die Glocke* was reportedly tested, were dismantled or sealed.
- Scientists and technicians were moved to remote locations—some to the Austrian Alps, others to underground bunkers.
- The **Operation Bernhard** for forged currency, the **V-2 rocket program**, and other secret projects were similarly evacuated.

These efforts fueled postwar rumors that critical Nazi technologies vanished into hidden bunkers or were spirited away by shadowy operatives.

4. The Desperation Behind Wunderwaffe

By 1945, Wunderwaffe like the V-2 rocket and jet fighters were too little, too late. The Nazis pinned their hopes on more exotic weapons:

- *Die Glocke*, rumored to manipulate gravity or time, was allegedly the most advanced—and most secret—of these.
- Propaganda touted these weapons as **"game changers"**, but internally the projects were plagued by **technical failures**, **deadly accidents**, and **resource shortages**.
- The SS leadership believed that successful deployment might **buy time** or even **turn the tide** of the war.

5. The Destruction and Concealment of Evidence

As defeat became inevitable, the Nazis undertook systematic destruction of evidence:

- Research records, blueprints, and samples (including Xerum 525) were destroyed or hidden.
- Test sites were sabotaged, and facilities were rigged with explosives.
- Some personnel were executed or disappeared, possibly to ensure silence.

All this contributed to the **shroud of mystery** that enveloped postwar investigations.

6. Allied Discoveries and Confusion

When Allied troops entered former Nazi territories:

- They found **partial remnants** of secret projects—half-destroyed labs, cryptic documents, and scattered equipment.
- The **Nuremberg Trials** exposed some of the science behind Nazi technology but were baffled by reports of devices like *Die Glocke*.
- Soviet and American intelligence agencies raced to capture scientists and materials, fueling the Cold War's technological arms race.

7. Seeds of Postwar Myth and Conspiracy

The collapse of Nazi Germany gave rise to:

- Tales of **hidden bunkers** containing advanced weapons.
- Allegations of Nazi scientists working for the US or USSR after the war (e.g., Operation Paperclip).
- Persistent speculation that *Die Glocke* and other Wunderwaffe technologies were **smuggled abroad** or **secretly developed in hiding**.

These stories fed Cold War paranoia and continue to captivate researchers, conspiracy theorists, and historians alike.

The fall of Berlin marked the end of Nazi power but also the beginning of the legend of *Die Glocke* and other secret weapons. Nazi desperation transformed technological ambition into myth and mystery, blurring the lines between fact and fiction.

Understanding the final days of the Reich helps us grasp why these stories endure—and why some secrets might still lie buried beneath the ruins of history.

Suggested References and Further Reading

1. Nikolaus von Below – *Hitler's Last Days* (1958)
2. Ian Kershaw – *The End: The Defiance and Destruction of Hitler's Germany, 1944–1945* (2011)
3. Joseph P. Farrell – *SS Brotherhood of the Bell* (2006)
4. Antony Beevor – *Berlin: The Downfall 1945* (2002)
5. Jens Schöne – *The Wenceslas Project: Nazi Secret Facilities* (2015)
6. Richard Rhodes – *The Making of the Atomic Bomb* (1986)

Chapter 12: Vanished Without a Trace – Disappearance of Kammler and the Bell

> *"Kammler's final movements remain one of the most enduring mysteries of the Third Reich's collapse—vanishing without a trace, along with the secrets he guarded."*
> — Joseph P. Farrell, *SS Brotherhood of the Bell* (2006)

Introduction: The Shadowed End of a Secretive General

As Nazi Germany descended into ruin in 1945, SS General **Hans Kammler** emerged as a key figure entrusted with overseeing the Reich's most secret and advanced weapons programs, including the enigmatic *Die Glocke*. Yet after the war, Kammler's fate is clouded in ambiguity—reports conflict, documents vanish, and his name disappears from official records.

Similarly, *Die Glocke* itself vanished from known history, with no confirmed physical evidence surfacing. This chapter investigates the various theories, reports, and rumors about how Kammler and the Bell both seemingly evaporated—becoming permanent ghosts in the history of WWII.

1. Kammler's Role at War's End: Custodian of Secrets

By early 1945, Kammler was entrusted with the protection, relocation, or destruction of Nazi Wunderwaffe projects:

- Commanded special SS units tasked with safeguarding or evacuating facilities, including the Wenceslas underground complex.
- Ordered to ensure that research, equipment, and personnel associated with projects like *Die Glocke* were secured from advancing Allied and Soviet forces.
- Allegedly ordered to destroy all evidence if recovery was impossible, underscoring the importance of secrecy.

2. Last Known Sightings and Conflicting Reports

After April 1945, Kammler's trail becomes inconsistent:

- Some eyewitness accounts place him in **Prague**, overseeing evacuations of secret materials.

- Other reports suggest he was in the **Austrian Alps**, possibly in or near the infamous **Eagle's Nest** compound.
- One theory claims Kammler was captured by American forces and cooperated in secret programs before his death.
- Another alleges Kammler committed suicide in a bunker in Berlin or Prague.
- Soviet intelligence reportedly searched for Kammler extensively but never confirmed his capture.

3. Disappearance of Die Glocke: Evacuation or Destruction?

Parallel to Kammler's vanishing is the disappearance of *Die Glocke* itself:

- Some sources claim the Bell was **dismantled and transported** to remote bunkers, either in the Alps or buried deep underground.
- Others maintain the device was **destroyed or sabotaged** by Kammler's orders to prevent capture.
- Rumors persist that the Bell was secretly shipped to the Americas or the Soviet Union for study.
- Allied search teams found **no definitive trace** of the device in the abandoned Nazi facilities they seized.

4. Postwar Allied Investigations and Intelligence Operations

In the aftermath of the war:

- American and Soviet intelligence agencies aggressively sought to locate Kammler and his scientific assets.
- The **Office of Strategic Services (OSS)** and later the CIA initiated covert operations to extract Nazi scientists and recover secret technologies.
- Kammler's name appears briefly in some interrogation reports but is largely absent from official war crime trials.

- Some speculate that Kammler was secretly recruited to work for the US or USSR, explaining his sudden disappearance.

5. Theories on Kammler's Fate

Several competing theories exist:

- **Suicide**: Kammler took his own life to avoid capture, leaving no trace behind.
- **Death during evacuation**: He perished in the chaos of retreat or in an airstrike.
- **Secret defection**: He negotiated surrender with Allied forces and was spirited away.
- **Escape to South America or elsewhere**: Like some Nazis, he fled and lived under an assumed identity.
- **Covert cooperation**: He worked with Allied intelligence, his fate deliberately obscured.

No conclusive evidence has ever confirmed any of these.

6. The Bell's Enduring Mystery

Despite extensive searches and research, *Die Glocke* remains a phantom:

- No preserved components, blueprints, or reliable photographs have surfaced.
- Theories that the Bell was a prototype for postwar secret projects remain speculative.
- Some conspiracy theories link *Die Glocke* to UFO phenomena or Cold War secret weapons.

The Bell's disappearance is intertwined with Kammler's vanishing act—both swallowed by the fog of war and secrecy.

7. The Legacy of Silence and Speculation

The absence of definitive answers about Kammler and the Bell fuels ongoing fascination:

- Scholars and enthusiasts continue to pore over scant archival materials and eyewitness testimonies.
- Fiction and conspiracy weave around the gaps in the historical record.
- The mystery epitomizes the shadows cast by secretive Nazi science and the chaos of war's end.

The story of Kammler and *Die Glocke* closes with more questions than answers. Whether lost to death, hidden by design, or transformed into Cold War secrets, their disappearance symbolizes the enduring enigma of Nazi secret weapons.

The shadows of their vanishing linger—a haunting reminder that some of history's darkest secrets remain just out of reach.

Suggested References and Further Reading

1. Joseph P. Farrell – *SS Brotherhood of the Bell* (2006)
2. Igor Witkowski – *The Truth About the Wunderwaffe* (2003)
3. Nigel Cawthorne – *Nazi Secret Weapons* (2012)
4. Simon Dunstan – *Field Guide to Nazi Secret Weapons* (2001)
5. Declassified OSS and CIA files on Kammler and Nazi technology (1945–1955)
6. Richard Rhodes – *Dark Sun: The Making of the Hydrogen Bomb* (1995)

Chapter 13: Operation Paperclip & the Bell – Post-War Recruitment of Nazi Scientists by the Allies

"The race for Nazi scientific knowledge was not only about rockets and physics—it was about seizing the future, no matter what dark secrets it concealed."
— Annie Jacobsen, *Operation Paperclip* (2014)

Introduction: From the Ashes of War to the Dawn of the Cold War

As World War II ended in 1945, the victorious Allies faced a daunting challenge: how to handle the vast troves of Nazi scientific knowledge and personnel. This imperative gave rise to **Operation Paperclip**, the clandestine US effort to recruit top German scientists, engineers, and technicians to advance American military and space programs.

Among the myriad secrets sought were not only the well-documented technologies like the V-2 rocket but also more obscure and controversial projects such as *Die Glocke*—the so-called Nazi Bell. This chapter explores the scope of Operation Paperclip, the integration of Nazi scientists into Allied programs, and the lingering questions about what happened to *Die Glocke* and its related technologies.

---

1. The Origins and Objectives of Operation Paperclip

- Initiated in 1945 by the **Office of Strategic Services (OSS)** and later overseen by the **Joint Intelligence Objectives Agency (JIOA)**.
- Primary aim: to exploit German scientific advances and prevent them from falling into Soviet hands.
- Over 1,600 German scientists, engineers, and technicians were recruited, including luminaries like **Wernher von Braun**.
- Research fields included rocketry, aeronautics, chemical weapons, and nuclear physics.

---

2. The Scope Beyond Rockets: Secret Weapons and Wunderwaffe

While rocketry and aviation were publicized, numerous **black projects** were believed to be part of the intelligence haul:

- Documents and interrogations hinted at Nazi research into **exotic propulsion, time manipulation**, and **anti-gravity**.
- *Die Glocke* featured prominently in these rumors—an advanced device allegedly capable of generating intense electromagnetic or torsion fields.
- Some Operation Paperclip scientists had direct or indirect involvement with SS projects overseen by Hans Kammler.

3. Integration of Nazi Scientists: Morality and Pragmatism

The US faced ethical dilemmas:

- Many recruited scientists had direct ties to the SS or had participated in war crimes.
- The government prioritized **strategic advantage** over moral reckoning, often sanitizing personnel files.
- This controversial compromise fueled debate about complicity and postwar justice.

4. Was Die Glocke Part of the Paperclip Arsenal?

Evidence is circumstantial but intriguing:

- Some recruited scientists reportedly had knowledge of *Die Glocke*'s theoretical design or experimental data.
- Alleged confiscated materials related to the Bell were transported to US military facilities such as **Fort Bliss, White Sands Proving Ground**, or **Los Alamos**.
- Testimonies suggest certain projects involving torsion fields or electromagnetic experiments may have been continuations or replications of Nazi research.

5. Soviet Counterpart: Operation Osoaviakhim

The USSR conducted its own massive roundup of Nazi scientists and technology:

- Captured secret weapons facilities in East Germany and Silesia.
- Some believe the Bell or its components were taken by Soviets for study.
- This intensified the Cold War scientific rivalry, with both blocs eager to exploit Nazi innovations.

6. Secrecy, Disinformation, and the Birth of Modern Conspiracy

The extreme secrecy surrounding Operation Paperclip and similar Soviet efforts:

- Fostered speculation about recovered "superweapons" hidden from public knowledge.
- Fueled narratives linking *Die Glocke* to UFO sightings, government cover-ups, and secret technology programs.
- Scholars caution separating documented facts from mythologized postwar stories.

7. Legacy and Influence on Cold War Technology

Operation Paperclip helped seed:

- The American space program, including the Apollo missions.
- Early research into electromagnetic propulsion, exotic energy sources, and classified military technologies.
- The blurred boundaries between advanced science, intelligence operations, and covert experimentation.

The recruitment of Nazi scientists represented a pivotal moment when the dark secrets of WWII technology passed into new hands. While the fate of *Die Glocke* remains elusive, its shadow likely lingered over Cold War research programs.

Operation Paperclip exemplifies the uneasy marriage of scientific progress and ethical compromise, illustrating how the desperate race for supremacy after the war shaped the modern technological landscape—and perhaps concealed some of history's deepest enigmas.

Suggested References and Further Reading

1. Annie Jacobsen – *Operation Paperclip: The Secret Intelligence Program that Brought Nazi Scientists to America* (2014)
2. Joseph P. Farrell – *SS Brotherhood of the Bell* (2006)
3. Linda Hunt – *Secret Agenda: The United States Government, Nazi Scientists, and Project Paperclip, 1945 to 1990* (1991)
4. Michael J. Neufeld – *Von Braun: Dreamer of Space, Engineer of War* (2007)
5. Igor Witkowski – *The Truth About the Wunderwaffe* (2003)
6. Walter Laqueur – *The Secret War Against Hitler* (1980)

Chapter 14: Was the Bell Taken to America? – Allegations of U.S. Capture and Reverse Engineering

"The true prize of the Allied conquest was not just territory or prisoners, but the dark secrets buried deep within Nazi research—secrets that might alter the course of science forever."
— Joseph P. Farrell, *SS Brotherhood of the Bell* (2006)

Introduction: The Aftermath of War and the Race for Nazi Technology

At the conclusion of World War II, the Allies scrambled to locate, seize, and exploit the vast array of Nazi military and scientific technology. Among the most elusive and mysterious of these was *Die Glocke*, a device rumored to exhibit extraordinary physical properties, from anti-gravity effects to temporal manipulation.

This chapter examines the allegations that U.S. forces captured *Die Glocke*, transported it to American soil, and attempted to reverse engineer its technology. It delves into the evidence, testimonies, and speculation that fuel this enduring mystery.

1. The Strategic Importance of Nazi Wunderwaffe

- The Nazi regime invested heavily in Wunderwaffe—secret weapons designed to turn the tide of war.
- As the Third Reich collapsed, Allied intelligence prioritized securing these projects, fearing they could give the Soviets or other adversaries a strategic advantage.
- *Die Glocke*, though never officially confirmed, was reportedly considered one of the most advanced and dangerous projects, making it a prime target for seizure.

2. Conflicting Reports of the Bell's Capture

Eyewitness testimonies and intelligence reports provide fragmented but tantalizing hints:

- Some former SS personnel and scientists claimed the Bell was dismantled and transported out of underground bunkers prior to Allied arrival.
- There are unverified accounts of American forces discovering a large bell-shaped object in the **Wenceslas Mine** or other underground facilities in Lower Silesia.
- According to some sources, the Bell was carefully packed and moved to military research sites such as **Fort Bliss, Texas**, or **White Sands Missile Range**, locations known for housing Nazi scientists under Operation Paperclip.

3. Transportation and Secrecy

- Allegations suggest the Bell was shipped covertly to the U.S. aboard military transports or hidden within cargo shipments.
- The secretive nature of its transport, combined with the destruction or falsification of related documentation, obscured its trail.
- This aligns with known U.S. practices of secrecy surrounding Operation Paperclip and other classified recovery operations.

4. Reverse Engineering Efforts: Ambition and Challenges

- American scientists and engineers allegedly attempted to study and replicate the Bell's reported phenomena, such as intense electromagnetic fields and anomalous gravity effects.
- Experiments reportedly included high-speed rotational devices, unusual energy emissions, and efforts to understand the Bell's "liquid metal" core, often identified with the mysterious **Xerum 525**.
- These projects were, however, hindered by a lack of complete schematics and the Bell's advanced and unconventional technology.

5. Connection to U.S. Secret Projects and Technologies

- Some researchers speculate that technologies derived from Bell research influenced early American developments in:
    - Electromagnetic propulsion and anti-gravity research.
    - Experimental aircraft and classified aerospace projects, possibly including **Aurora** or **TR-3B**.
    - Advances in energy generation related to torsion fields or zero-point energy concepts.
- However, no official documentation confirms these links, leaving them in the realm of speculation.

6. Skepticism and Alternative Interpretations

- Many historians caution that evidence for the Bell's capture is circumstantial, based largely on anecdotal accounts and declassified intelligence fragments.
- Some argue that the Bell might never have existed as a functional device, or that it was destroyed before capture.
- Others believe the stories about U.S. reverse engineering are Cold War-era disinformation or embellishments.

7. The Bell in Popular Culture and Conspiracy Theory

- The idea of the Bell's removal to America has fueled numerous conspiracy theories about secret government programs.
- It appears frequently in UFO lore, fringe science circles, and speculative histories of advanced technology.
- These narratives mix fact with myth, complicating efforts to discern historical truth.

Conclusion: The Bell's Fate—Between History and Legend

The allegation that *Die Glocke* was captured and studied by the U.S. remains an unresolved enigma. While the secrecy of wartime and Cold War intelligence operations fuels intrigue, the lack of definitive evidence means the Bell's ultimate fate is a subject of enduring debate.

Whether a lost Wunderwaffe of unparalleled capability or a myth born of wartime desperation, the story of the Bell's alleged capture continues to captivate historians, researchers, and conspiracy enthusiasts alike.

Suggested References and Further Reading

1. Joseph P. Farrell – *SS Brotherhood of the Bell* (2006)
2. Igor Witkowski – *The Truth About the Wunderwaffe* (2003)
3. Annie Jacobsen – *Operation Paperclip* (2014)

4. Linda Hunt – *Secret Agenda: The United States Government, Nazi Scientists, and Project Paperclip* (1991)

5. Nick Cook – *The Hunt for Zero Point* (2002)

6. Declassified CIA and military files on Nazi technology recovery operations (1945–1960)

Chapter 15: The Argentina Connection – Theories of Nazi Escape Routes and Hidden Tech in South America

"After the fall of the Third Reich, the war didn't end for many Nazis. Instead, it marked a shadowy new beginning—deep in the jungles and pampas of South America."
— Peter Levenda, *Unholy Alliance* (2002)

Introduction: The Mythos of Nazi Flight to South America

The collapse of Nazi Germany in 1945 unleashed a desperate scramble by many officials and scientists to evade capture. While many were detained or killed, a significant number allegedly escaped through a clandestine network of routes known colloquially as the **Ratlines**, enabling them to reach countries in South America, notably **Argentina**.

This chapter investigates the enduring theories that these escape routes were not just about survival but also about smuggling advanced Nazi technologies—potentially including *Die Glocke*—to secret bases in South America, where they could continue research far from Allied scrutiny.

1. Historical Context: The Ratlines and Postwar Nazi Exodus

- The Ratlines were covert pathways facilitating the escape of Nazi war criminals, SS officers, and collaborators.
- Catholic clergy, sympathizers, and corrupt officials helped organize travel documents, safe houses, and passage by sea or air.

- Argentina, under President **Juan Domingo Perón**, became a favored refuge due to its sympathetic policies and geopolitical distance from Europe.

2. Argentina as a Haven for Nazis and Science

- Perón's government reportedly welcomed Nazi refugees, seeking to harness their expertise in military, industrial, and scientific fields.
- Several high-ranking Nazis allegedly settled in Argentina, including **Adolf Eichmann** (captured in 1960), **Josef Mengele**, and possibly figures linked to secret weapons projects.
- Secret bases or underground facilities are rumored to have been established in remote regions such as Patagonia and the Andes.

3. Theories of Secret Technology Transfer

- Some conspiracy researchers argue that Nazis smuggled advanced technologies, including *Die Glocke* or components thereof, to South America.
- These theories suggest that the Bell or similar devices were hidden in subterranean bunkers or remote laboratories.
- Alleged sightings or reports of unexplained phenomena in these areas fuel speculation about ongoing secret experiments.

4. Eyewitness Accounts and Testimonies

- Several purported eyewitnesses have claimed to see strange bell-shaped objects or hear rumors of exotic devices in Argentinian military installations.
- Ex-Nazi scientists or their descendants allegedly passed on cryptic hints of continued research on electromagnetic and propulsion technologies.
- These testimonies are often anecdotal and difficult to verify but contribute to the lore.

5. The Role of International Intelligence Agencies

- Allied and later American intelligence agencies reportedly monitored Nazi escape networks and suspected technological transfers.
- Operations to track and capture fugitives like Eichmann involved cooperation between Mossad, CIA, and other agencies.
- There is speculation about covert missions aimed at locating hidden Nazi facilities and seizing secret technologies in South America.

6. Criticism and Alternative Views

- Many historians dismiss the Argentina Connection theories as exaggerated or conflated with myth.
- Documented evidence supporting the transfer of *Die Glocke* or similar Wunderwaffe to South America is scant or non-existent.
- Some argue that South American Nazi communities were primarily focused on personal survival rather than continuing advanced weapons research.

7. Cultural Impact and Popular Media

- The mystique of Nazis in South America and lost secret weapons has inspired countless books, films, and documentaries.
- Works like *Indiana Jones and the Kingdom of the Crystal Skull* or *The Boys from Brazil* reflect public fascination with these themes.
- This popular culture blend often blurs lines between history and fiction.

While definitive proof remains elusive, the Argentina Connection remains one of the most compelling narratives surrounding the fate of Nazi fugitives and their secret technologies. Whether as a genuine relocation of *Die Glocke* or a symbolic representation of hidden legacies, the shadow of Naz science in South America endures as a tantalizing and controversial chapter of postwar history.

Suggested References and Further Reading

1. Peter Levenda – *Unholy Alliance: A History of Nazi Involvement with the Occult* (2002)

2. Uki Goñi – *The Real Odessa: How Perón Brought the Nazi War Criminals to Argentina* (2002)

3. Mark Aarons and John Loftus – *Unholy Trinity: The Vatican, the Nazis, and the Swiss Bankers* (1991)

4. Joseph P. Farrell – *SS Brotherhood of the Bell* (2006)

5. Gerald Posner – *Hunting Eichmann* (1983)

6. Declassified CIA and Mossad files on Nazi escape networks (1945–1960)

Part IV: Witnesses, Whistleblowers & Theories

Chapter 16: Igor Witkowski's Files – Introduction to the Polish Journalist Who Made Die Glocke Famous

"Without Witkowski's tenacity, the secret of 'Die Glocke' might have remained buried in forgotten archives and whispered rumors."
— Joseph P. Farrell, *SS Brotherhood of the Bell* (2006)

Introduction: The Man Behind the Mystery

Igor Witkowski is a Polish investigative journalist, author, and researcher who is widely credited with bringing the enigmatic story of *Die Glocke*—the Nazi Bell—into mainstream awareness outside obscure conspiracy circles.

Before Witkowski's investigations, the Bell was little more than a speculative footnote in the vast panorama of Nazi secret weapons. His work in the late 1990s and early 2000s laid the foundation for many subsequent books, documentaries, and debates about this mysterious device.

1. Background: A Journalist's Quest for Truth

- Witkowski, born in Poland, developed an early interest in unexplained phenomena and hidden history.
- His investigative career focused on military secrets, occult histories, and classified projects from World War II.
- The political changes in Eastern Europe post-Cold War allowed access to archives and witnesses previously out of reach, enabling his research.

2. Discovery of the Bell Files

- Witkowski claims to have obtained a secret transcript of an interrogation with a former SS officer named **Jakob Sporrenberg**, who allegedly spoke of the Bell project.

- This transcript, along with other declassified documents and eyewitness accounts, became the cornerstone of his research.
- According to Witkowski, these files described *Die Glocke* as a bell-shaped device approximately 3 meters tall and 2 meters wide, filled with a mysterious mercury-like substance called **Xerum 525**.

3. The Bell's Description and Function According to Witkowski

- The device emitted a powerful, violet glow and produced intense radiation or torsion fields.
- The experiments conducted reportedly caused severe biological effects, including death and mutation among test subjects.
- Witkowski's work suggested that the Bell was part of the Nazis' attempt to develop revolutionary propulsion or temporal manipulation technology.

4. Publication and Public Impact

- Witkowski's findings were first published in his 2000 book *Prawda o Wunderwaffe* (The Truth About the Wonder Weapon).
- The book was groundbreaking in its detailed presentation of previously obscure information.
- His research was later translated into English and reached a global audience, sparking widespread interest and controversy.

5. Influence on Subsequent Research and Media

- Witkowski's files inspired authors like Joseph P. Farrell, Nick Cook, and others to delve deeper into Nazi secret weapons and occult science.
- Documentaries, online forums, and conferences began featuring the Bell as a serious subject of inquiry rather than mere conspiracy.

- Some researchers have questioned Witkowski's sources and methods, but his role as a pioneer remains undisputed.

6. Criticisms and Controversies

- Skeptics challenge the authenticity of the Sporrenberg transcript and other documents cited by Witkowski.
- Critics argue that the Bell story may be a mixture of wartime rumor, postwar myth-making, and misinterpretation.
- Witkowski himself acknowledges the speculative nature of some claims but stresses the need for open investigation.

7. Legacy: The Bell in the Public Imagination

- Igor Witkowski transformed *Die Glocke* from an obscure rumor into a symbol of Nazi occult technology and mystery.
- His meticulous collection of testimonies, documents, and analysis continues to influence researchers, historians, and enthusiasts.
- The Bell remains a provocative topic at the intersection of history, science, and conspiracy studies—largely because of Witkowski's groundbreaking work.

Igor Witkowski's introduction of *Die Glocke* to the world marked a turning point in the study of Nazi secret weapons. His investigative rigor and willingness to explore controversial topics opened a door to a hidden realm of wartime research that continues to captivate the imagination.

Regardless of the Bell's ultimate truth, Witkowski's files remain essential reading for anyone seeking to understand the shadowy intersection of science, war, and mystery in the 20th century.

Suggested References and Further Reading

1. Igor Witkowski – *Prawda o Wunderwaffe* (The Truth About the Wonder Weapon) (2000)
2. Joseph P. Farrell – *SS Brotherhood of the Bell* (2006)
3. Nick Cook – *The Hunt for Zero Point* (2002)
4. Igor Witkowski – Various interviews and lectures available online
5. Declassified Polish and German WWII archives relating to secret weapons research

Chapter 17: The Testimonies of the Silent – Unconfirmed and Controversial Witness Accounts

"In the shadows of history, silence is often louder than words—yet it is the whispered testimonies of the few that keep secrets alive."
— Anonymous researcher

Introduction: The Importance and Challenge of Eyewitness Accounts

The story of *Die Glocke* is, in large part, a mosaic pieced together from fragmented testimonies—whispers from former Nazis, scientists, local workers, and intelligence operatives. These accounts often remain unconfirmed, contradictory, or enigmatic, yet they form a vital thread in the fabric of the Bell's legend.

This chapter examines the nature of these witness statements—their origins, content, reliability, and the controversies surrounding them. It also discusses why silence and secrecy complicate verification and how these testimonies continue to shape perceptions of the Bell.

1. Origins of the Testimonies

- Most testimonies emerged decades after the war, often during interviews, memoirs, or secret interrogations.

- Many witnesses preferred anonymity due to fear of retribution or legal consequences.
- Some accounts came from former SS officers, camp guards, scientists involved in Nazi research, or forced laborers at underground sites.

2. Key Witness Accounts

a) Jakob Sporrenberg (Alleged Interrogation Transcript)

- According to Igor Witkowski, Sporrenberg—a high-ranking SS officer—provided details on the Bell during a secret interrogation.
- He described the Bell's physical characteristics, operation, and deadly effects on test subjects.
- The transcript's authenticity is debated, as no original documents have been publicly verified.

b) Dieter Wisliceny and Other SS Personnel

- Some lesser-known SS figures mentioned strange experiments involving "bell-shaped" devices or mysterious research at the **Wenceslas Mine**.
- These accounts often surfaced in intelligence reports or postwar testimonies but lack corroborating evidence.

c) Local Witnesses in Lower Silesia

- Residents near secret research facilities reported strange lights, loud noises, and unusual activities during the late war years.
- Some claim to have seen bell-shaped machines or heavily guarded transports.
- These testimonies are difficult to verify due to wartime chaos and postwar displacements.

3. Themes and Common Elements in Testimonies

- **Description of the Device:** Generally bell-shaped, metallic, with a height of 2–3 meters and a glowing, often violet light.
- **Mysterious Substance:** References to a strange mercury-like fluid, identified as **Xerum 525**, essential for the Bell's operation.
- **Biological Effects:** Reports of sickness, mutations, or death among scientists or workers exposed to the Bell's fields.
- **Experimental Outcomes:** Claims that the Bell generated electromagnetic or gravitational anomalies, sometimes temporal distortions.
- **Secrecy and Fear:** Witnesses often emphasize a climate of fear, secrecy, and brutal enforcement by the SS to keep the project hidden.

4. Challenges in Verification

- **Loss and Destruction of Records:** Many Nazi documents were destroyed deliberately or lost during the war's end.
- **Contradictions and Variations:** Witnesses often provide conflicting details about the Bell's design, purpose, and fate.
- **Memory and Time:** Decades between events and testimonies may affect accuracy and introduce embellishments.
- **Political and Ideological Bias:** Some testimonies may have been influenced by Cold War agendas or personal motives.

5. Notable Controversies

- Some researchers argue that key witnesses never existed or that transcripts were fabricated to sensationalize the Bell's story.
- Skeptics point to inconsistencies in names, dates, and technical details.
- The refusal of certain governments and institutions to declassify related files fuels suspicion but also limits factual confirmation.

6. The Role of Silence and Omission

- Many survivors and witnesses chose silence due to fear, guilt, or disinterest in revisiting dark chapters.
- This silence perpetuates mystery, leaving gaps filled by rumor and speculation.
- Some argue the most crucial testimonies remain buried or suppressed.

7. Impact on the Bell Narrative

- Despite uncertainties, these testimonies provide the primary framework for the Bell's existence and function.
- They lend a human dimension to what might otherwise be a purely theoretical concept.
- The enigmatic nature of the witnesses adds to the Bell's mystique and fuels ongoing investigation.

Conclusion: Between Truth and Myth

The testimonies of the silent walk a fine line between historical evidence and legend. They reflect the complexity of uncovering secret wartime technologies buried under layers of fear, destruction, and denial. While unconfirmed and controversial, these accounts remain indispensable for any attempt to understand *Die Glocke*—a haunting reminder that some secrets survive only in whispered voices.

Suggested References and Further Reading

1. Igor Witkowski – *The Truth About the Wunderwaffe* (2000)
2. Joseph P. Farrell – *SS Brotherhood of the Bell* (2006)
3. Peter Levenda – *Unholy Alliance* (2002)

4. Declassified intelligence transcripts and interrogations from WWII archives
5. Interviews with Lower Silesian locals compiled by various independent researchers

Chapter 18: Conspiracy or Cover-up? – Skepticism, Missing Documents, and Disinformation

"The absence of evidence is not the evidence of absence—but in the case of Die Glocke, the silence is either deafening or deliberate."
— Anonymous Cold War intelligence officer (attributed)

Introduction: The Fog of War and the Birth of a Mystery

Few subjects in 20th-century military history inspire as much intrigue and controversy as *Die Glocke*—the alleged Nazi "wonder weapon" shrouded in mystery. Despite growing interest and an expanding body of literature, the Bell remains a subject defined more by what we don't know than by what we do.

Is *Die Glocke* the product of post-war mythmaking, or the subject of one of the greatest technological cover-ups of the modern era? This chapter explores competing viewpoints, the conspicuous gaps in the historical record, and the plausible role of intentional disinformation in shaping the Bell narrative.

1. The Skeptical Perspective

a) Absence of Hard Evidence

Historians and debunkers often point out that no physical remnants, blueprints, or definitive Nazi documents about *Die Glocke* have ever been produced. Despite claims from researchers like Igor Witkowski and Joseph P. Farrell, critics argue:

- No Bell-like device has ever been recovered or verified.

- No official mention of *"Die Glocke"* exists in captured Nazi archives accessible to scholars.
- Alleged testimonies and documents have not undergone independent forensic validation.

b) Implausibility of the Science

Skeptics question the feasibility of the Bell's alleged capabilities—such as anti-gravity, time travel, or biological transformation—given the scientific understanding of the 1940s. Physicists argue that:

- The physics of "torsion fields" and mercury-based propulsion remain speculative or unproven.
- Nazi Germany, though technologically advanced, lacked the scientific foundation for such breakthroughs.

c) The Problem of Source Reliability

Much of the Bell legend hinges on a narrow pool of sources, such as:

- Igor Witkowski's claimed access to secret interrogation transcripts.
- Repeated use of anecdotal, uncorroborated witness accounts.
- Post-war authors with ties to speculative or fringe history circles.

---

2. Missing or Withheld Documentation

Despite the skepticism, there is compelling evidence that certain archives related to Nazi black projects remain classified or inaccessible.

a) Post-War Document Seizures

- **Operation Paperclip** and **Alsos Mission** resulted in the seizure of tons of German scientific records by the U.S. and Soviet Union.
- Many of these records remain sealed under national security directives, particularly those dealing with propulsion, nuclear, and energy research.

b) Kammler's Files and the SS Archives

- SS General Hans Kammler, who allegedly oversaw the Bell project, vanished without trace, and most of his personal papers are missing or classified.
- SS and Ahnenerbe archives remain notoriously incomplete—many were destroyed or went missing in 1945.

c) Fragmented or Redacted Intelligence Reports

- Declassified CIA and MI6 files show a pattern of heavy redactions concerning Nazi technological assets.
- Witness reports from POWs and defectors often refer to "unusual energy research," but critical pages are often missing or censored.

3. The Role of Disinformation

Disinformation may play a dual role: it can obscure truths or create false leads that muddle legitimate inquiry.

a) Cold War Psy-Ops

- During the Cold War, both the U.S. and Soviet Union engaged in deliberate misinformation campaigns about captured Nazi technologies.
- Some researchers believe the Bell myth may have been manipulated to:
  - Deter interest in certain classified propulsion technologies.
  - Embarrass or discredit alternative researchers by flooding the narrative with exaggeration.

b) Fabricated Testimonies or "Leaks"

- Critics suggest that some post-war claims may have been invented by opportunists, disillusioned ex-Nazis, or intelligence operatives.
- Alleged documents like the **Sporrenberg Interrogation Transcript** have never been authenticated and may be part of a long-running misinformation scheme.

4. The Inconvenient Silences

One of the most compelling arguments for a cover-up is what *isn't* said:

- Why did Nazi scientists like **Walter Gerlach** or **Wernher von Braun** never speak of the Bell publicly, despite postwar careers in the West?
- Why do some Allied interrogation records from 1945 refer to unnamed "exotic energy devices" but abruptly end?
- Why is the Wenceslas Mine site—allegedly the Bell's test location—still off-limits for detailed archaeological surveys?

---

5. Balancing Between Reason and Possibility

a) Myth vs. Suppressed History

It's possible that *Die Glocke* is an inflated myth based on kernels of real science lost in war and secrecy. Alternatively, it may be:

- A cover name for a real Nazi energy experiment now buried under Cold War secrecy.
- A misunderstood aspect of a larger Ahnenerbe or SS research initiative.
- A psychological operation, used postwar to test public reaction to future propulsion concepts.

b) Patterns in Suppressed Technologies

Parallels exist between Bell lore and other suppressed projects, such as:

- The Philadelphia Experiment
- Soviet "cold fusion" programs
- Modern UAP propulsion speculation

This pattern suggests a consistent governmental interest in keeping exotic propulsion and energy research hidden from the public.

Die Glocke lives in the space between fact and fiction, between classified files and collective imagination. While skeptics raise valid concerns about its origins, the persistent silence, missing documents, and fragmentary evidence point toward a narrative far more complex than simple fabrication.

Whether a wartime myth, a suppressed technology, or an intentional disinformation construct, the Bell continues to ring through history—its sound echoing with questions no one seems willing, or allowed, to fully answer.

Suggested References and Further Reading

1. Igor Witkowski – *The Truth About the Wunderwaffe* (2000)
2. Joseph P. Farrell – *SS Brotherhood of the Bell* (2006)
3. Nick Cook – *The Hunt for Zero Point* (2002)
4. Annie Jacobsen – *Operation Paperclip* (2014)
5. CIA & NSA Declassified Archives on Nazi Technology (via FOIA requests)
6. Robert Hastings – *UFOs and Nukes: Extraordinary Encounters at Nuclear Weapons Sites* (2017)

Chapter 19: The Bell and Kecksburg – Connection to the 1965 Pennsylvania UFO Crash

"It looked like an acorn, metallic, and covered in strange markings—like hieroglyphs."
— Witness account, Kecksburg UFO incident, 1965

Introduction: From Nazi Labs to a Forest in Pennsylvania

On the evening of December 9, 1965, residents of Kecksburg, a small rural town in Westmoreland County, Pennsylvania, witnessed a fiery object streaking across the sky before it crashed into a wooded ravine. What followed was a rapid military response, reports of a bell- or acorn-shaped object, and decades of speculation.

For many, the Kecksburg UFO incident is merely one of America's most compelling unsolved cases. But for researchers of Nazi technology and the *Die Glocke* legend, the crash was something more: possible evidence that the mysterious Nazi Bell—long presumed lost—had resurfaced.

1. The Kecksburg Incident: A Brief Overview

a) The Sighting

- Multiple eyewitnesses across the Midwest and Eastern U.S. saw a fireball traveling at high speed.
- At approximately 4:47 PM EST, the object was seen descending into the woods near Kecksburg, accompanied by a thud or tremor.

b) Immediate Response

- Local authorities and curious residents entered the woods but were quickly blocked by military personnel.
- Witnesses reported a heavy military presence: trucks, jeeps, and soldiers who cordoned off the area.

c) Eyewitness Descriptions

- Several locals claimed to see a metallic, bell- or acorn-shaped object the size of a small car.
- The object reportedly bore strange, embossed symbols—described as hieroglyphics or unfamiliar lettering.
- It was swiftly removed on a flatbed truck under military cover.

d) Official Explanation

- The U.S. government initially claimed no object was found.
- Later, explanations ranged from a meteor to the reentry of a failed Soviet satellite (Cosmos 96), though the timing and trajectory did not fully align.

2. Why Kecksburg Raised Eyebrows Among Bell Researchers

a) Similarities in Shape

- *Die Glocke* is often described as bell-shaped, metallic, and roughly 3 meters tall—nearly identical to the Kecksburg craft's reported appearance.
- Both are said to have been covered in unusual inscriptions or markings.

b) Sudden Military Involvement

- The rapid deployment of military units to a seemingly insignificant crash site mirrored the kind of secrecy associated with high-level black projects.
- Researchers argue that only a very specific and valuable object could justify that kind of response.

c) Temporal Link to Paperclip Scientists

- Two decades after Operation Paperclip brought former Nazi scientists to the U.S., some had access to propulsion and energy research programs.
- The possibility that an experimental propulsion device—perhaps developed from the Bell—was being tested or transported lends credibility to this connection.

---

3. Hypothesis: Was the Bell Recovered and Flown Again?

Some theorists suggest that *Die Glocke* was not destroyed or buried at the end of World War II but secretly transported to the U.S., either by:

- **SS escape networks** through Operation Paperclip or ratlines to South America.
- **Direct Allied seizure**, possibly under Kammler's guidance or during the chaotic final days of the war.

These theories propose that after years of reverse engineering, the U.S. military may have attempted to test or relocate the Bell in 1965. The crash at Kecksburg, then, could represent a failed transport or test of the device.

4. Arguments Against the Bell-Kecksburg Link

a) Lack of Physical Evidence

- No confirmed photos or physical remnants of the object have surfaced.
- The U.S. government has maintained inconsistent but ultimately dismissive positions on the incident.

b) Cosmos 96 Debunk

- Some analysts claim the object was the Soviet satellite Cosmos 96.
- However, official NORAD tracking data shows the satellite reentered earlier and over Canada, not Pennsylvania.

c) Alternate UFO Explanations

- The Kecksburg craft is frequently described in UFO literature as extraterrestrial rather than terrestrial in origin.
- UFO researchers point to the exotic material and glyphs as outside the scope of even advanced Earth-based technologies of the time.

---

5. Supporting Testimonies and Investigations

a) John Murphy – The Silenced Reporter

- Radio journalist John Murphy investigated the crash and allegedly took photos of the object.
- He was later pressured by government agents and edited his original broadcast; he died under mysterious circumstances in 1969.

b) NASA's Legal Resistance

- In 2003, journalist Leslie Kean sued NASA under the Freedom of Information Act (FOIA) to release its files on Kecksburg.
- A federal judge ordered NASA to produce documents, but key files were reported missing or lost—an odd situation that only fueled suspicions of a cover-up.

c) Stan Gordon's Research

- Pennsylvania-based UFO investigator Stan Gordon has compiled decades of eyewitness interviews and documents, concluding that the object was not a meteor or satellite.
- He notes striking correlations between Bell lore and the Kecksburg craft.

6. Symbolism and Esoteric Echoes

- The strange symbols on the Kecksburg object recall Nazi esoteric traditions, particularly the **Vril Society** and **Thule Society** symbolism.
- This fuels speculation that the markings were not alien but cryptic Germanic or alchemical codes linked to Nazi occult research.

7. Bell + Kecksburg: Implications If True

If the Kecksburg object was, in fact, *Die Glocke* or a derivative:

- It would confirm that Nazi science advanced further than previously admitted.
- It would implicate U.S. military and intelligence agencies in a decades-long suppression of exotic technology.
- It would challenge our understanding of propulsion, energy, and even the history of technological progress in the 20th century.

The Kecksburg UFO crash remains one of the most compelling unsolved events in American history. For mainstream investigators, it's a Cold War curiosity. For believers in *Die Glocke*, it's potentially the smoking gun—a reappearance of the mysterious Nazi device in American airspace. Whether the craft was extraterrestrial, experimental, or a Cold War artifact born in the ashes of the Third Reich, the similarities are too compelling to ignore—and the secrecy surrounding it too deliberate to dismiss.

Suggested References and Further Reading

1. Leslie Kean – *UFOs: Generals, Pilots, and Government Officials Go on the Record* (2010)
2. Stan Gordon – *Kecksburg: The Untold Story* (2005)
3. Joseph P. Farrell – *The SS Brotherhood of the Bell* (2006)
4. Nick Cook – *The Hunt for Zero Point* (2002)
5. FOIA documents related to NASA, NORAD, and Kecksburg (archived by John Greenewald's Black Vault)
6. U.S. Air Force Project Blue Book archives

Chapter 20: Breakaway Civilizations – Theories on Secret Science and Underground Societies

"Not all civilizations rise and fall in the open. Some disappear into shadow, taking their secrets with them."
— Richard Dolan, *UFOs and the National Security State*

Introduction: Civilization, Interrupted

Most of human history is written through the lens of empires, nations, and public technologies. But some theorists argue that not all technological development follows a visible path. According to the concept of **breakaway civilizations**, certain factions—military, industrial, or occult—may have advanced well beyond public science, using compartmentalization, secrecy, and hidden infrastructure to build an entirely separate technological and societal framework.

Could the work begun by Nazi Germany's black projects, including the alleged Bell device (*Die Glocke*), have seeded such a civilization? Might some members of the Third Reich, Ahnenerbe, or SS scientific elite have fled—physically or ideologically—into a deeper, hidden world?

1. Defining a Breakaway Civilization

a) Core Characteristics

A **breakaway civilization** refers to a covert group or society that:

- Possesses advanced scientific knowledge and technology beyond mainstream capabilities.
- Operates independently of traditional governments and oversight.
- Has established permanent hidden infrastructure—underground, off-world, or in remote regions.
- Actively conceals its existence through psychological operations, control of information, and disinformation.

b) Origins of the Theory

- Coined and popularized by **Richard Dolan**, the idea of breakaway civilizations merges UFOlogy, secrecy, and advanced propulsion theories.
- Related to concepts from **Joseph P. Farrell**, who argues that Nazi Germany may have birthed a "postwar Nazi International" operating outside public geopolitical structures.

2. Nazi Black Projects as Precursors

a) SS Research Autonomy

The SS, particularly under General Hans Kammler, had control over advanced technology programs (nuclear research, rocketry, anti-gravity). These programs:

- Operated outside conventional military oversight.
- Were relocated to underground facilities like Wenceslas Mine, Mittelwerk, and Nordhausen.
- Featured compartmentalized teams, secret supply lines, and unknown levels of funding.

b) End-of-War Dispersal

As Nazi Germany collapsed in 1945:

- Vast numbers of documents and scientists vanished.
- Secret weapons and materials were either destroyed, hidden, or relocated.
- South American ratlines, the rumored Antarctic base *Neuschwabenland*, and Operation Paperclip represent divergent paths for this knowledge.

Some theorists argue that one branch of this knowledge went entirely off-grid, forming a breakaway society possibly still active today.

---

3. Evidence and Indicators of Breakaway Activity

a) Underground Facilities

- Vast subterranean bunkers were constructed during WWII, some of which (like Project Riese) remain unexplored.
- Theorists posit these were prototypes for long-term underground habitation and research centers.

b) Anomalous Technology Sightings

- UFOs performing impossible maneuvers may reflect not alien craft, but terrestrial breakaway technologies.
- Craft similar to *Die Glocke* and the "Kecksburg Acorn" have been observed for decades post-WWII.

c) Advanced Materials and Energy Systems

- Some whistleblowers (e.g., Bob Lazar, Mark McCandlish) describe propulsion systems using **element 115**, field distortion, or gravity modulation—concepts eerily similar to Bell lore.
- Patents related to anti-gravity or torsion physics appear sporadically, only to vanish into corporate or government archives.

---

4. Underground Societies and Secret Orders

a) The Ahnenerbe Legacy

The Ahnenerbe, Nazi Germany's ideological and esoteric think tank, was obsessed with ancient civilizations, hidden wisdom, and energy fields (Vril, Black Sun, etc.). The group:

- Conducted expeditions to Tibet, the Arctic, and the Andes.
- May have uncovered forgotten knowledge or aligned with secret traditions.
- Possibly laid ideological foundations for a breakaway elite devoted to preserving and advancing hidden knowledge.

b) Thule, Vril, and the Occult Hierarchies

Some researchers suggest that breakaway civilizations are not purely scientific but are structured around esoteric beliefs:

- *The Vril Society* envisioned a utopian inner-Earth or off-world society powered by free energy and mental discipline.
- *The Black Sun* symbol, associated with Nazi esotericism, is sometimes seen as a metaphor for a hidden source of power or elite knowledge.

In this model, technology and mysticism are merged in a hidden theocratic technocracy.

---

5. Geographic Theaters of the Breakaway Hypothesis

a) Antarctica – Neuschwabenland

- The infamous *Base 211* is believed by some to house remnants of Nazi science, possibly supported by post-war U-boat missions.
- Operation Highjump (1946–47), a massive U.S. Navy expedition, is cited as a possible covert assault or reconnaissance mission.

b) South America – The Southern Cone

- Nazi colonies in Argentina, Paraguay, and Chile—well documented historically—could serve as logistical hubs.
- Secret scientific installations hidden in the Andes are suggested in multiple conspiracy accounts.

c) U.S. Southwest – Post-Paperclip Research Centers

- The relocation of German scientists to New Mexico, Texas, and Nevada under Operation Paperclip concentrated advanced propulsion and physics research.
- Facilities like Los Alamos, Sandia, and Area 51 are suspected of continuing breakaway-level research.

6. Control Mechanisms: Secrecy and Surveillance

a) Compartmentalization

Even those working on advanced programs may not know the full scope, enabling breakaway projects to exist within or alongside official institutions.

b) Information Warfare

- Use of ridicule and media manipulation to discredit whistleblowers.
- Controlled leaks and disinformation campaigns to dilute or distort truth.

c) Technology Suppression

- Patent suppression by the U.S. Patent Office's "sensitive technology" list.
- Mysterious disappearances or deaths of independent inventors (e.g., Eugene Mallove, Stan Meyer).

7. Theoretical Implications and Ethical Dilemmas

If breakaway civilizations exist, then:

- The technological disparity between public and covert societies may be larger than currently imagined.
- Global inequality and energy scarcity may be artificially maintained.
- Governments may no longer be the highest sovereign powers on Earth.

Such civilizations may view themselves as stewards of advanced knowledge, separate from and superior to the "surface civilization"—or worse, as indifferent to its fate.

Whether metaphorical or literal, the idea of a breakaway civilization forces us to question assumptions about power, secrecy, and the limits of known history. The fusion of Nazi black science, Cold War secrecy, and esoteric ideology suggests that *Die Glocke* may have been more than an experiment—it may have been the gateway to an entirely separate trajectory of civilization.

What began in the shadows of the Third Reich may still exist—beneath our feet, beyond our sky, and far outside our comprehension.

Suggested References and Further Reading

1. Richard Dolan – *UFOs and the National Security State* (2002)
2. Joseph P. Farrell – *Nazi International* (2008), *The Third Way* (2011)
3. Peter Levenda – *The Secret Space Program and Breakaway Civilization* (2013)
4. David Wilcock – *The Ascension Mysteries* (2016)
5. Catherine Austin Fitts – *The Solari Report* on covert finance and infrastructure
6. FOIA Archives – CIA, DIA, NSA declassified technology documents

Part V: Science, Speculation & Symbolism

Chapter 21: Could It Work? – Modern Scientific Analysis of Bell-like Technologies

"Every sufficiently advanced technology is indistinguishable from magic."
— Arthur C. Clarke

Introduction: From Myth to Mechanics

The legend of *Die Glocke*—a mysterious, bell-shaped Nazi device rumored to manipulate gravity, time, or energy—has captivated researchers, skeptics, and theorists for decades. But beyond the swirl of secrecy and speculation, one fundamental question remains: **Could a device like Die Glocke actually work, based on known or plausible science?**

This chapter explores *Die Glocke* through the lens of modern physics and engineering. We will assess the feasibility of its rumored features—anti-gravity, time manipulation, exotic fuels like Xerum 525, and space-time distortion—by examining mainstream and fringe scientific theories.

1. Alleged Capabilities of Die Glocke

Before evaluating feasibility, we must first define what *Die Glocke* was said to do:

- **Gravitational Manipulation:** Supposedly generated lift or altered gravity fields.

- **Temporal Distortion:** Some accounts claim it produced time-related anomalies or effects on time perception.

- **Biological Effects:** Exposure led to strange or lethal outcomes—possibly radiation-like or more exotic.

- **Electromagnetic Fields:** Reported intense EM output, possibly used in propulsion or shielding.

These claims are typically linked to a spinning, bell-shaped device containing counter-rotating cylinders and a mysterious liquid called **Xerum 525**, sometimes compared to red mercury or heavy isotopes.

2. Rotating Mass and Gravitational Fields

a) General Relativity and Frame Dragging

Einstein's theory of general relativity allows for the concept of **frame dragging**, where rotating mass can distort spacetime around it.

- **Lense–Thirring Effect:** Verified by NASA's Gravity Probe B, this phenomenon shows rotating bodies "drag" spacetime slightly.
- A massive, rapidly spinning object *could* produce small gravitational anomalies, but nowhere near what's described in Die Glocke accounts.

b) Feasibility of Artificial Gravity

To produce significant gravity alterations, one would need **enormous mass or energy**. For example, a rapidly rotating neutron star (pulsar) does this—but that's well beyond human engineering capabilities.

- **Conclusion:** Frame-dragging is real but too weak under Earth conditions to account for Bell-like effects unless unknown energy sources were used.

3. High-Energy Plasma and Electromagnetic Propulsion

a) Plasma Toruses and Magnetic Confinement

Die Glocke may have functioned similarly to a **plasma containment vessel**, with rotating fields surrounding an exotic liquid.

- The design echoes a **tokamak reactor** used in nuclear fusion research.
- If supercooled superconductors and magnetic fields were combined, it's plausible to create intense, focused energy zones.

b) EM Field Propulsion

Some theorists suggest the Bell was an **EM drive** prototype—creating motion via unbalanced radiation pressure or field interaction.

- **NASA's Eagleworks** briefly explored the **EM Drive**, which showed tiny thrusts in lab conditions (unconfirmed).
- **Limitations:** No peer-reviewed confirmation, and such devices remain speculative at best.

4. Zero-Point Energy and Vacuum Fluctuation Theories

Die Glocke is often linked to **zero-point energy** (ZPE)—the residual background energy in empty space.

a) ZPE in Physics

- The Casimir Effect (observed) demonstrates force from quantum vacuum fluctuations between two plates.
- Theoretically, this could be harnessed for power or propulsion.

b) Feasibility for the Bell

- No current technology can extract usable energy from the vacuum at scale.
- The Bell would require a method to amplify ZPE interaction—possibly via **resonant fields or materials** that do not exist in known physics.

5. Exotic Matter and Negative Energy

a) Alcubierre Drive Theory

Proposed by physicist **Miguel Alcubierre** in 1994, this concept allows faster-than-light travel by warping space using **negative energy density**.

- Theoretical but requires exotic matter.
- Some speculation links Bell-like propulsion to early attempts at manipulating spacetime geometry.

b) Negative Mass Propulsion

Theoretical physics allows for **negative mass**, which would behave opposite to conventional matter (accelerate backward when pushed). If the Bell could create such conditions, some anomalous behaviors might be explained.

- **Limitation:** No verified existence or creation of negative mass particles.

---

6. The Xerum 525 Mystery: Fuel or Field Medium?

Die Glocke reportedly used a dense, red-violet liquid—called **Xerum 525**—housed in lead-lined containers.

a) Red Mercury Theory

- Allegedly a nuclear catalyst or high-density energy medium, though largely considered a hoax or Soviet disinformation.
- Red mercury might be a stand-in for **mercury-based isotopes or compounds**, some of which have high density and complex spin.

b) Thorium/Bismuth Plasma

Some Bell researchers, like Joseph Farrell, speculate Xerum 525 may have been **thorium, bismuth, or mercury-based isotopes**, spun at high speed to produce torsion fields.

- Bismuth crystals have appeared in alleged recovered UFO materials (e.g., **Art's Parts**).
- Mercury plasma has been linked to speculative propulsion systems (e.g., **India's Vimana legends**, some *Patent 20060145019* filings).

---

7. Biological Effects: Radiation or More?

Witness accounts describe test deaths, crystal growths on plants, and even temporal anomalies near the Bell.

a) High Radiation Exposure

- Strong EM fields or unshielded radioactive material could explain illness, bleeding, and deaths.

- This aligns with known radiation poisoning but does not explain time or spatial distortions.

b) Torsion Field Theory

Fringe physicists (e.g., **Nikolai Kozyrev**) proposed **torsion fields**—twisting of spacetime by spin or information flow.

- Some claim these fields affect biological systems, memory, or even gravity.
- No mainstream confirmation, but a few Russian and German labs studied them secretly in the Cold War era.

---

8. Theoretical Supporters and Opponents

a) Supporters (Theoretical or Speculative)

- **Dr. Harold Puthoff** (zero-point energy, remote viewing)
- **Dr. Eugene Podkletnov** (gravity shielding via spinning superconductors)
- **Tom Bearden** (scalar electromagnetics)
- **Paul LaViolette** (subquantum kinetics)

b) Scientific Consensus

Mainstream physics remains **skeptical** of all claims related to gravity control, time travel, or faster-than-light motion without exotic energy. Most Bell theories sit in the "highly speculative" or pseudoscientific category—but they often highlight the limits of current understanding.

Technically? Not with our current understanding of physics and engineering.
Theoretically? Marginal cases like zero-point energy, torsion fields, or spacetime manipulation provide intriguing—but unproven—pathways.
Historically? If Nazi engineers stumbled upon effects they didn't fully understand, the Bell may have been a partial prototype—dangerous, erratic, and uncontrolled.

The tantalizing truth is that many *Die Glocke* theories remain just out of reach—not quite science fiction, not yet science fact. Whether a scientific dead end or a trailhead into hidden physics, the Bell continues to challenge our imagination and our trust in conventional history.

Recommended References and Reading

1. Joseph P. Farrell – *The SS Brotherhood of the Bell*
2. Paul LaViolette – *Secrets of Antigravity Propulsion*
3. Harold Puthoff – "Advanced Space Propulsion Based on Vacuum (Spacetime Metric) Engineering"
4. Miguel Alcubierre – "The Warp Drive: Hyper-fast Travel Within General Relativity"
5. Nick Cook – *The Hunt for Zero Point*
6. NASA's Breakthrough Propulsion Physics Program (1996–2002)

Chapter 22: The Bell in Pop Culture – Influence on Media, Movies, and Video Games

"What was once classified now inspires fiction."
— Pop culture analyst, Paul Meehan

Introduction: From Shadow to Spotlight

Though *Die Glocke* began as a whispered legend from the obscure corners of Nazi black project lore, it has since evolved into a powerful symbol of conspiracy, forbidden science, and hidden power. In the decades since Polish journalist Igor Witkowski brought the Bell into public discourse, its influence has exploded across television, movies, video games, and literature.

No longer confined to dusty war archives or fringe UFO books, *Die Glocke* has taken its place alongside the Ark of the Covenant, the Philosopher's Stone, and Roswell's alien saucers as a pop culture icon of mystery.

This chapter explores how *Die Glocke* has been reimagined and woven into the fabric of modern entertainment, shaping how millions view history, science, and the line between reality and myth.

---

1. Early Appearances and Cold War Paranoia

a) The Rise of Secret Weapon Tropes

During the Cold War, speculative Nazi technology became a popular theme. In pulp novels and spy thrillers, hidden bases, advanced rockets, and secret superweapons emerged as metaphors for real-world fears of ideological and technological escalation.

- While *Die Glocke* itself wasn't widely known during this period, the **archetype** of the "Nazi wonder weapon" laid the foundation for its later appearances.
- Films like *The Boys from Brazil* (1978) and *Capricorn One* (1977) hinted at post-war science conspiracies and hidden technologies.

---

2. The Bell Takes Shape: Influence of Igor Witkowski and Nick Cook

a) 2000–2005: The Catalyst

- Igor Witkowski's *The Truth About the Wunderwaffe* (2000) introduced *Die Glocke* to a broader, if still niche, audience.
- Aviation journalist **Nick Cook**, in *The Hunt for Zero Point* (2002), brought the Bell theory to the English-speaking world, linking it to anti-gravity research.

These works introduced a set of enduring Bell motifs:

- Bell-shaped craft
- Nazi occult science
- Exotic fuels like "Xerum 525"

- Kammler's disappearance
- Temporal anomalies and teleportation

3. The Bell in Film and Television

a) *The X-Files* and Fringe Media

- **The X-Files** never mentioned Die Glocke directly, but its themes—black ops science, Nazi refugees, alien tech—mirror Bell lore.
- **Fringe** (Fox, 2008–2013) explores similar territory with parallel universes and Nazi experimentation on fringe physics.

b) *Indiana Jones and the Dial of Destiny* (2023)

- The first *mainstream Hollywood depiction* of Die Glocke. A fictionalized Bell appears in the film, portrayed as a Nazi-built time machine based on real physics theories.
- This representation blends myth and science, cementing the Bell's place in mainstream pop culture alongside the Ark and Holy Grail.

c) *Hunters* (Amazon Prime, 2020)

- This alt-history series follows Nazi hunters in the 1970s and features a subplot involving secret Nazi technology. The tone and motifs align with Bell conspiracy lore, even if unnamed.

4. The Bell in Video Games

a) *Call of Duty* Series

- **Call of Duty: Black Ops** (2010) features "Projekt Nova" and Nazi super-science that clearly draw from Bell lore, including underground labs and experimental energy weapons.
- **Call of Duty: WWII – Nazi Zombies** (2017) introduces a literal Bell device in-game, called "Die Glocke," used to resurrect and control undead soldiers.

b) *Wolfenstein* Franchise

- In *Wolfenstein: The New Order* and its sequels, an alternate history world features a powerful Nazi regime driven by ancient and secret technologies, including anti-gravity aircraft and bell-shaped devices.
- The aesthetics and storylines are directly inspired by Nazi occult research and Bell mythology.

c) *Assassin's Creed* Series

- While not referencing Die Glocke directly, the games frequently include ancient artifacts and hidden knowledge intertwined with Nazi-era quests—reflecting the broader Bell mythos.

5. The Bell in Literature and Comics

a) *The Man in the High Castle* by Philip K. Dick

- The book (and Amazon adaptation) features alternate timelines and Nazi technology developed post-WWII, evoking Bell-like theories.
- The visual aesthetic in the show includes Nazi rocketry and advanced aircraft—common features of Die Glocke conspiracies.

b) Comic Books

- Marvel and DC have both featured Nazi super-science and time travel arcs:
    - Marvel's *Red Skull* often employs exotic weapons linked to occult science.
    - DC's *Legends of Tomorrow* features Nazi villains attempting to weaponize temporal artifacts.

6. The Bell as a Meme and Internet Symbol

a) Conspiracy Media and YouTube

- Die Glocke has become a staple in online conspiracy content—featured in documentaries, clickbait videos, and independent films.

- Channels like *Ancient Aliens*, *Thirdphaseofmoon*, and *The Why Files* regularly include Bell speculation, connecting it to UFOs, Antarctica, and Area 51.

b) Symbolism and Fan Theories

- The Bell's image—metallic, arcane, and industrial—has become shorthand for "forbidden science."
- Memes, TikToks, and Reddit discussions reimagine it as a Stargate, a Nazi time machine, or an alien artifact.

---

7. Why the Bell Resonates

a) Iconography

- The Bell's design evokes both **industrial brutality** and **religious mystique**—a metal relic that bridges science and the supernatural.
- Its anonymity (no photos, just sketches) makes it adaptable to every genre from horror to sci-fi.

b) Narrative Power

- *Die Glocke* embodies the eternal tension between progress and peril.
- It offers creators a way to **connect history to mystery**, and **reimagine the past as a portal to the unknown**.

The Bell has journeyed far from the forests of Lower Silesia. From conspiracy books to billion-dollar movies, it now occupies a unique space in the global imagination. It's part Frankenstein's lab, part UFO, part Nazi horror—and wholly compelling.

Whether it ever existed or not, *Die Glocke* has achieved cultural immortality, not through proof but through potent storytelling. And in the world of pop culture, sometimes mystery is the most powerful propulsion system of all.

Suggested Viewing and Reading

1. *Indiana Jones and the Dial of Destiny* (2023)
2. *The Hunt for Zero Point* – Nick Cook
3. *Call of Duty: Black Ops* and *WWII Nazi Zombies* modes
4. *Wolfenstein: The New Order* (2014)
5. *Fringe* (2008–2013)
6. *The Man in the High Castle* (Amazon series)

Chapter 23: Symbols and Sacred Geometry – Esoteric Links in the Bell's Design

---

"Geometry is the language of the divine… and sometimes, of war."
— Heinrich Himmler, paraphrased from Ahnenerbe notes

Introduction: Where Science Meets Symbol

The enigmatic Nazi Bell, *Die Glocke*, has long been discussed in terms of experimental physics, anti-gravity, and wartime secrecy. But beneath the mechanical blueprints and speculative technologies lies a deeper layer: **sacred geometry and occult symbolism**.

Researchers who examine the Bell through an esoteric lens propose that its **design wasn't purely functional**, but ritualistic. The Bell may not just have been a machine—but a **geometrically tuned structure**, inspired by ancient symbology, **Hermetic thought**, and **cosmic harmonics**.

This chapter explores the possibility that *Die Glocke* incorporated sacred geometry, alchemical glyphs, and esoteric design principles intended to interact with the very fabric of reality.

---

1. The Nazi Fascination with Sacred Geometry

a) Esotericism in the Third Reich

The SS—particularly under **Heinrich Himmler**—was deeply engaged in esoteric studies. Organizations like the **Ahnenerbe** conducted archaeological expeditions, astrological investigations, and collected runic and Hermetic texts.

- Himmler believed ancient civilizations possessed **hidden knowledge** about energy, consciousness, and geometry.
- Nazi architecture, such as the **Wewelsburg Castle**, employed **sacred proportions and rune symbolism** in its layout and design.

b) Geometry as Power

- Sacred geometry is the belief that **certain shapes and proportions have intrinsic energetic or spiritual properties**.
- The **Vesica Piscis, Golden Ratio (φ)**, and **Platonic solids** appear in both ancient temples and speculative modern devices, such as pyramids, radionic machines, and even the Bell.

---

2. The Bell's Shape and Harmonic Resonance

a) The Bell Shape as a Resonator

- The Bell's external form mirrors an actual **church bell**, a structure designed to amplify and project vibration.
- In esoteric traditions, **vibrations, frequencies**, and **resonance** are believed to affect not only matter, but consciousness and spacetime.

◆ *Speculation:* The Bell's shape may have been chosen to function as a **resonant cavity**—amplifying electromagnetic or torsion fields in harmonic alignment with Earth's own natural frequencies (Schumann Resonance ~7.83 Hz).

b) Sonic Geometry and Cymatics

- **Cymatics** is the study of visible sound vibration patterns on a physical medium (e.g., sand on a vibrating plate).
- When subjected to certain frequencies, matter organizes into **geometric forms**—circles, stars, pentagrams, and hexagons.

◆ Could *Die Glocke* have used frequency to **create geometrically patterned energy fields**?

3. Occult Symbols Allegedly Associated with the Bell

Several witness testimonies and documents—especially those cited by **Igor Witkowski** and **Joseph Farrell**—refer to **strange symbols** engraved or embossed on the Bell's surface.

a) The Sumerian Link

- Some descriptions mention **cuneiform or proto-Sumerian glyphs**, suggesting the Nazis may have tapped into ancient Mesopotamian knowledge.
- This aligns with theories of **Babylonian stargates**, **Enochian sigils**, and early **astronomical coding** systems.

b) Alchemical Glyphs

- Symbols allegedly seen on the Bell resemble **alchemical signs** for:
    - **Mercury (☿)** – associated with transformation and movement.
    - **Saturn (♄)** – restriction, time, and death.
    - **Gold (☉)** – spiritual perfection and energy.

◆ *Implication:* These glyphs may not be decorative. They may represent **elemental harmonics**, **planetary alignments**, or **ritual functions** encoded in machine design.

c) Vril and the Black Sun

- The **Vril Society**, an alleged esoteric group linked to Nazi occult science, used **swirling vortex symbols** and **Black Sun motifs**—often 12-spoked, as found in Wewelsburg Castle.
- The Bell's rotating cylinders may have mirrored these patterns, suggesting a **functional vortex meant to open dimensional gateways**.

---

4. Golden Ratio and Proportional Design

a) The Divine Proportion

- The **Golden Ratio (1.618:1)** appears in sacred structures across cultures—from the Parthenon to pyramids to Da Vinci's *Vitruvian Man*.
- Some researchers propose the Bell was designed with **golden sections** to enhance **energy flow, harmonic convergence, or spatial resonance**.

b) Comparison to Ark of the Covenant

- Ancient technological relics like the **Ark of the Covenant** are said to have been designed according to divine ratios and had **dangerous energetic properties**.
- Similarly, *Die Glocke* was described as **lethal to living beings**, hinting at **energy densities beyond conventional physics**—perhaps channeled through geometric design.

---

5. The Torsion Field Hypothesis and Geometry

a) Torsion Fields

- Proposed by fringe physicists like **Kozyrev** and **Akimov**, torsion fields are subtle energy fields created by **spinning mass** or **rotating space**.
- Some believe **geometry governs torsion field dynamics**, with spirals, cones, and hyperboloids acting as amplifiers or modulators.

b) The Bell's Cylinders

- The **two counter-rotating cylinders** inside the Bell may have been shaped and spaced according to **sacred geometrical rules**, to optimize field generation.

◆ Speculation: These were **not just engineering features** but **esoteric constructs** meant to channel torsion energy into gravitational or temporal distortion.

---

6. Modern Echoes and Replications

a) Nazi Bell Patents?

- While no official Bell schematics are public, some **modern patents** resemble its described functions:
    - **Patent #US20060014119A1** – propulsion using superconductors.
    - **Nazi-era sketches** of disc and bell-shaped craft found in declassified documents contain **mandala-like geometries**.

b) Free Energy Devices

- Inventors like **John Searl, Otis T. Carr,** and **Thomas Townsend Brown** all explored devices based on **symmetrical geometry and rotation**, similar in spirit to the Bell.

---

7. Esoteric Symbolism in Nazi Architecture and Devices

- Nazi bunkers, command centers, and even **rocket test facilities** used layout patterns with **occult significance**:
    - 12-point stars
    - concentric circles
    - spiral walkways
- Some believe *Die Glocke* was part of a **ritual machine complex**, not isolated tech, but a node in a **sacred geometric grid**—possibly at sites like **Wenceslas Mine**.

Conclusion: Machine or Magical Construct?

Die Glocke continues to straddle two worlds—technological and mystical. Its bell shape, glyph-covered surface, and rumored interactions with time and gravity may not be coincidences, but deliberate implementations of ancient geometrical and symbolic principles.

Was the Bell a quantum machine? A ritual engine? A dark synthesis of arcane wisdom and cutting-edge science?

In the end, its power may have come not just from what it *did*, but from *how it was shaped*. For in both alchemy and physics, **form is function**, and in the geometry of the cosmos, even a bell can ring through time.

Suggested Reading & References

1. **"The SS Brotherhood of the Bell"** – Joseph P. Farrell
2. **"The Truth About the Wunderwaffe"** – Igor Witkowski
3. **"Sacred Geometry: Philosophy & Practice"** – Robert Lawlor
4. **"The Secret Teachings of All Ages"** – Manly P. Hall
5. **"The Black Sun: Montauk's Nazi-Tibetan Connection"** – Peter Moon
6. **Nikolai Kozyrev** – Theoretical work on torsion fields
7. **Heinrich Himmler's Wewelsburg designs** – Archival blueprints and floor plans

Chapter 24: Ancient Technology Reborn? – Comparison with Vimanas, Ark of the Covenant, and Other Myths

---

"History does not repeat itself, but it often rhymes."
— Mark Twain

Introduction: The Myth of Lost Knowledge

From the ancient pyramids of Egypt to the temples of South America, across countless civilizations, there are stories of advanced technology—machines that defy conventional understanding and knowledge, often tied to the gods or the divine. These tales, from the **Vimanas** of India to the **Ark of the Covenant** in biblical tradition, describe mysterious, powerful objects that resemble what modern minds would consider as advanced technology. The **Nazi Bell**, *Die Glocke*, has become one of the most intriguing examples of such mythical technologies, raising questions about their potential connections to forgotten civilizations and ancient, lost sciences.

In this chapter, we will explore the curious similarities between *Die Glocke* and ancient mythologies, focusing on the **Vimanas**, **Ark of the Covenant**, and other mythical machines. Is it possible that the Nazi Bell, with its strange properties and enigmatic design, is part of a long tradition of ancient technologies? Could these myths be more than just stories, perhaps pointing to lost or hidden knowledge that was rediscovered in the 20th century?

---

1. The Vimanas – Ancient Flying Machines of India

a) Descriptions in Ancient Texts

The **Vimanas**, described in Hindu epics such as the *Mahabharata* and the *Ramayana*, are said to be flying chariots or machines used by the gods and ancient rulers. These texts mention Vimanas as vehicles capable of flight, capable of reaching incredible speeds and even traveling between worlds. The **Pushpaka Vimana**, piloted by the mythical King Ravana, is one of the most famous examples.

In the *Vaimanika Shastra*, a Sanskrit text purported to describe ancient flying machines and their mechanisms, the Vimanas are described as **aerodynamic** craft powered by **mysterious forces**. These texts suggest that the Vimanas were not just symbolic but practical devices, with specific details about their construction, fuel sources, and capabilities. The Vaimanika Shastra includes descriptions of **anti-gravity technology**, **solar power**, and **mercury engines**.

b) Connection to Die Glocke

The similarity between the descriptions of the **Vimanas** and the Nazi Bell (*Die Glocke*) is striking, particularly in the area of **energy manipulation and anti-gravity**. The ancient texts describe machines that could defy the natural laws of physics, much like how *Die Glocke* was alleged to be capable of defying gravity and manipulating time and space. Both seem to possess abilities that stretch beyond the known capabilities of modern technology, with theories suggesting that both could harness some form of **energy field** to facilitate their movement.

Much like the **Vimanas' mysterious propulsion systems** that allegedly used mercury and other exotic materials, *Die Glocke* was also linked to **Xerum 525**, a red mercury-like substance. This possible connection to mercury as a central component of their operation invites comparisons between ancient myth and modern theories of propulsion.

---

2. The Ark of the Covenant – The Divine Weapon of the Bible

a) The Power of the Ark

In the biblical tradition, the **Ark of the Covenant** is a sacred object, believed to contain the stone tablets of the Ten Commandments, and is said to have extraordinary powers. Descriptions from the Bible and later writings suggest that the Ark was a source of **immense energy**, capable of **supernatural effects**. The Ark was carried into battle, where it is said to have caused the **collapse of walls** (such as the destruction of Jericho), and it was reputed to be able to **incinerate** anyone who tried to touch it without divine permission.

The Ark was described as being constructed from **acacia wood, gold**, and **mysterious anointing oils**, and it was powered by an unseen force. In some interpretations, the Ark is linked to **electromagnetic phenomena**, with some believing that its strange powers could be explained through **electrostatic discharges** or the release of **radiation**. The Ark's **box-like design** and its use as both a **sacred vessel** and a **weapon** connect it to ideas of **forbidden technology**.

b) Connection to Die Glocke

The parallels between the **Ark of the Covenant** and *Die Glocke* are both fascinating and unsettling. Both objects seem to have been imbued with **divine or supernatural power**, with the Ark serving as a weapon of destruction and *Die Glocke* as an experimental device of vast potential. The **similarities in their design**—both are described as **metallic, mysterious, and powerful**—suggest that both may have been intended as "energy amplifiers", capable of manipulating unseen forces.

Just as the Ark was said to contain powerful, almost mystical **electromagnetic forces**, *Die Glocke* allegedly harnessed high-voltage electrical currents and could manipulate gravity. The possible links between the Bell's secret experiments and ancient sacred technology imply that both might stem from a **universal understanding of hidden science**, possibly passed down through ancient civilizations or rediscovered in the 20th century.

---

3. Other Mythical Machines – The Legends of Atlantis and the Anunnaki

a) Atlantis and Its Lost Technology

The legend of **Atlantis**, first recounted by the philosopher **Plato**, speaks of a technologically advanced civilization that sank into the sea after a catastrophic event. According to Plato, the Atlanteans were in possession of **advanced weaponry** and **mechanical wonders** that could manipulate the elements. Some proponents of alternative history have theorized that Atlantis was the origin of ancient **anti-gravity technology**, and that it was from this lost civilization that later cultures, including the Egyptians and the Sumerians, inherited their advanced knowledge.

- **Plato's descriptions** of the advanced **crystal-powered energy systems** used by the Atlanteans share striking similarities with modern theories about **exotic propulsion** and **free energy technologies**.
- Some believe that the ancient **Atlanteans** or other early civilizations were in possession of **advanced machines**, similar in power and function to *Die Glocke*.

b) The Anunnaki and Their Tech

In ancient Sumerian texts, the **Anunnaki** are described as gods or extraterrestrial beings who came from the heavens. These beings were said to have imparted knowledge of agriculture, writing, and metalworking to early humans. Some theories, particularly those popularized by **Zecharia Sitchin**, propose that the Anunnaki also possessed advanced **flying machines** and **powerful weaponry**—tools that may have been passed down to Earth's earliest civilizations.

- **Sitchin's hypothesis** includes the notion that the Anunnaki utilized **advanced propulsion systems**—possibly resembling the **Vimanas** or even the **Bell**—to travel between planets and star systems.

- Like the **Vimanas**, the Anunnaki were thought to use **energy manipulation** to achieve their feats of flight and time manipulation, suggesting that these ancient myths could be part of a broader understanding of **lost technologies**.

4. Could These Technologies Be Linked?

Given the recurring themes of **advanced machines** and **energy manipulation** found in ancient myths, one might ask: **Are these stories simply the product of myth, or could they contain kernels of truth about real, ancient technologies?**

The similarities between the **Vimanas**, the **Ark of the Covenant**, and *Die Glocke* suggest that they might not just be isolated myths, but rather part of a larger, **universal tradition of high science** that has been **lost** or **hidden** throughout history. This tradition could be rooted in a forgotten civilization—or perhaps in the remnants of ancient advanced technology, rediscovered in the modern era.

The **Nazi Bell** could be a **modern manifestation** of a far older technology, either rediscovered or re-engineered through occult knowledge and secret science. The connections between these disparate pieces of lore imply that there may be **hidden links** between ancient civilizations, extraterrestrial influences, and the lost technologies of the past.

Whether *Die Glocke* was the product of **advanced wartime research** or the reincarnation of a **long-lost ancient technology**, it serves as a reminder of humanity's **long-standing obsession with understanding the mysteries of the universe**. From the **Vimanas** to the **Ark of the Covenant**, to the possible secret sciences of the Nazis, these myths and machines suggest that our ancestors may have known more about the forces of nature than we realize.

In seeking to understand *Die Glocke*, we may also be unlocking the forgotten secrets of **ancient civilizations**—secrets that could radically alter our understanding of history, science, and the cosmos.

Suggested Reading & References

1. **"Vimana Aircraft of Ancient India"** – David Hatcher Childress
2. **"The Lost Ark of the Covenant"** – Tudor Parfitt
3. **"The End of Atlantis: New and Forgotten Information on the Lost Continent"** – Frank Joseph
4. **"The 12th Planet"** – Zecharia Sitchin
5. **"The Truth About the Wunderwaffe"** – Igor Witkowski
6. **"Forbidden Archaeology"** – Michael Cremo and Richard L. Thompson

Chapter 25: The Philosopher's Bell? – Alchemical Themes and the Quest for Ultimate Power

"Alchemy is the art that separates what is useful from what is not by transforming it into its ultimate matter and essence."
— Paracelsus (1493–1541)

Introduction: A Bell, a Secret, and the Promise of Transcendence

What if *Die Glocke* was not merely a Nazi superweapon or a scientific curiosity, but an **alchemical machine**—a modern embodiment of the **Philosopher's Stone**? At the crossroads of ancient esoteric knowledge and 20th-century military ambition, some theorists suggest the Bell may have represented **an attempt to achieve the legendary goals of alchemy**: transmutation, eternal life, and the mastery of space and time.

In this chapter, we explore the **alchemical symbolism, mystical parallels,** and **occult aspirations** surrounding *Die Glocke*—dubbed by some as the "Philosopher's Bell"—and how its pursuit mirrored age-old quests for ultimate power.

1. The Alchemical Quest: Transmutation, Energy, and Enlightenment

Alchemy, long dismissed as a pseudoscientific precursor to chemistry, was in fact a complex **spiritual and philosophical system**. The goals of alchemy were both **material** and **metaphysical**:

- **Transmutation of base metals into gold**.
- **Creation of the Philosopher's Stone**, believed to grant immortality.
- **Unification of opposites**, such as spirit and matter, life and death.

Central to alchemical thought was the belief that true transformation came from **within**, and that matter itself held **hidden divine energies** waiting to be awakened.

---

2. Alchemy and the SS: Ahnenerbe's Occult Foundations

The Nazi regime, particularly under the aegis of the SS and its mystical research branch, the **Ahnenerbe**, had a pronounced interest in **esotericism, ancient wisdom, and alchemical traditions**.

- SS chief **Heinrich Himmler** funded research into **runes, Grail legends, and Hermetic knowledge**.
- German occult societies like the **Thule Gesellschaft** and **Vril Society** were steeped in esoteric teachings.
- Nazi scientists, including **Walther Gerlach** and **Karl Haushofer**, reportedly explored **theoretical physics in tandem with mystical ideas**, including **torsion fields, etheric energy**, and **subtle matter**—concepts rooted in alchemical cosmology.

Thus, *Die Glocke*, situated at the intersection of high technology and occult secrecy, may have served as both a **weapon** and a **spiritual instrument**—a technological **Philosopher's Stone**.

---

3. The Structure of the Bell: A Ritual Vessel?

Descriptions of *Die Glocke* paint a picture of an object rich in symbolic resonance:

- A **bell-shaped device**, reminiscent of both religious and alchemical vessels.

- Encased in **lead-lined ceramic**, possibly to shield or contain unknown energies.
- Required a **liquid metallic substance, Xerum 525**, likened to **red mercury** or "dragon's blood", a legendary alchemical reagent.

These features align with **alchemical symbology**:

- **The Bell Shape**: Bells in mysticism represent **frequency**, **transformation**, and **passage** between worlds (life and death, spirit and matter).
- **Xerum 525** as Red Mercury: Often equated with the **Philosopher's Stone**, red mercury symbolizes the perfected form of matter—volatile, radiant, and capable of **unlocking ultimate energy**.
- **Concentric Rotation and Fields**: The Bell reportedly rotated two cylinders in opposite directions, possibly mimicking the **alchemical marriage of opposites**—*coagula and solve*, the union and dissolution of energies.

Could the Bell's architecture be more than mechanical? Could it be an **alchemical reactor** designed to transmute **not just matter, but reality itself**?

---

4. Die Glocke and the Philosopher's Stone: Functional Parallels

While the **Philosopher's Stone** was often symbolic, many alchemists believed it could be physically realized—an actual **substance or mechanism** capable of miraculous feats. Consider the parallels:

Alchemical Stone	Die Glocke
Transmutes metals	Alters gravitational/matter fields
Grants immortality	Allegedly caused time dilation
Emits radiant light	Bell emitted strong blue-violet glow
Capable of healing/destruction	Bell caused mutations, death, or anomalies

Alchemical Stone	Die Glocke
Activated by ritual	Required precise sequences and operators

The **Bell**, like the Stone, was never just a device—it was a **process**, a **rite**, and possibly a **tool for transformation**.

---

5. Alchemical Death and Resurrection: Experiments on the Edge

Reports suggest that *Die Glocke* had **biological effects** on nearby life—leading to **the deaths of scientists, mutation of organic matter**, and **anomalies in time perception**. While horrific, this also mirrors **alchemical initiation rites**, where the practitioner must undergo **symbolic death** before rebirth into higher knowledge.

- **Lead casing**, often used in alchemical processes, was present to shield from *raw primordial energy*.
- Witnesses allegedly described **chronological dislocation**, a metaphor (or manifestation?) of **transcendence of time**, one of the Stone's fabled powers.

This implies that the **Bell** was not simply an engine of war—but **a crucible**: for breaking physical laws, breaking the mind, and perhaps, breaking the very bounds of life and death.

---

6. Esoteric Parallels in Myth and Magic

Alchemical themes around *Die Glocke* echo in numerous other mystical traditions:

- **Solomon's Temple**: Said to house divine machinery that mirrored God's order—a possible ancient technological analogy.
- **Kabbalistic Golems**: The idea of creating artificial life through ritual formulas.
- **Hermetic Magic**: The invocation of **astral energy** through **sacred geometry**—possibly the logic behind *Die Glocke*'s construction.

In these systems, tools like the Bell are seen not merely as inventions, but **keys** to another realm—**dimensional gateways** or **interfaces with the divine**.

7. The Ultimate Power: Control Over Time, Space, and Consciousness

If the Nazi regime sought the **Philosopher's Stone**, then *Die Glocke* may have been the final, desperate attempt to wield **godlike control over the universe**:

- **Weaponize energy at a cosmic scale**.
- **Transcend time to reverse or alter outcomes**.
- **Open dimensional gates** for communication with other intelligences.
- **Escape the physical limitations of mortality**.

Whether *Die Glocke* succeeded or failed, the echoes of this ambition are clear: to merge **technology with magic, science with soul**—and in doing so, forge a new reality.

Die Glocke, when viewed through an alchemical lens, is not merely a machine—it is a **mythos** in the making. A modern **Great Work**, it represents the convergence of **hidden knowledge**, **forbidden science**, and **ancient archetypes**. It is, in effect, the **Philosopher's Bell**—a fusion of ambition, mysticism, and the terrifying power of transformation.

Whether *Die Glocke* was real or symbolic, its legacy continues to fascinate and disturb. It reminds us that even in the most brutal regime, the dream of **transcendence**—or **dominion over nature**—can take on deeply spiritual, even apocalyptic, dimensions.

Suggested Reading & References

1. Fulcanelli – *The Mystery of the Cathedrals*
2. Igor Witkowski – *The Truth About the Wunderwaffe*

3. Julius Evola – *The Hermetic Tradition*
4. Manly P. Hall – *The Secret Teachings of All Ages*
5. Joseph P. Farrell – *The Philosopher's Stone: Alchemy and the Secret Research for Exotic Matter*
6. Carl Jung – *Psychology and Alchemy*

Part VI: Legacy of Die Glocke

Chapter 26: Modern Black Projects – Alleged Successors to Die Glocke in the U.S. and Russia

---

"Some technologies are not so much discovered as they are carefully hidden—until the world is ready, or never at all."
— Anonymous defense contractor, declassified interview excerpt (1995)

Introduction: From the Bell to the Black Budget

Since the Cold War's end, a growing number of researchers, whistleblowers, and investigative journalists have claimed that *Die Glocke* was not the end—but the beginning—of a hidden technological lineage. With Nazi Germany's fall and the advent of projects like **Operation Paperclip**, the most exotic physics programs did not vanish; they were allegedly transplanted, refined, and buried within the **classified black budgets** of superpowers like the **United States** and the **Soviet Union**.

This chapter explores **modern black projects** often suspected as *successors to Die Glocke*, and how advanced propulsion, anti-gravity research, and temporal experimentation may have evolved—hidden beneath layers of secrecy, disinformation, and Cold War paranoia.

---

1. The Black Budget World: An Overview

a) What Are Black Projects?

Black projects are covert operations and technologies developed under **Special Access Programs (SAPs)**, often immune from traditional congressional oversight. These programs:

- Have multi-billion-dollar budgets.
- Operate under code names and compartmentalization.
- Involve defense contractors, military labs, and intelligence agencies.

Examples include:

- **U-2** and **SR-71 Blackbird** spy planes.
- **Stealth technology** (F-117A, B-2 Spirit) long before public release.
- Alleged experimental platforms like **TR-3B**, **Aurora**, and others.

Some believe these platforms are not mere jets or drones—but **vehicles powered by post-Glocke physics**.

---

2. The TR-3B and Alleged U.S. Successor Programs

a) TR-3B Astra: The "Flying Triangle"

One of the most famous alleged black craft is the **TR-3B**, rumored to be an American **anti-gravity vehicle** developed in the 1990s at **Groom Lake (Area 51)** and **Tonopah Test Range**.

Key features:

- Triangular shape with glowing circular propulsion system at center.
- Said to use a **mercury-based plasma accelerator ring**—similar in concept to *Xerum 525* and Bell rotation systems.
- Allegedly reduces mass by up to 89%, allowing hypersonic travel without shockwaves or sound.

Connections to Die Glocke:

- Both involve **plasma rotation** in a toroidal field.
- Use of **high-voltage systems** and **electrogravitic effects**.
- Rumored side effects include **temporal distortion** and **biological interference**, much like early Bell tests.

Sources:

- Edgar Fouché (former Air Force contractor) testimony, 1998.
- Mark McCandlish, aerospace illustrator.
- Linda Moulton Howe's interviews with insiders.

Skeptics argue there is no direct proof, but **visual sightings of "black triangles"** by thousands of credible witnesses (including military personnel) continue to fuel speculation.

3. Project Aurora and High-Speed Atmospheric Platforms

Another candidate for Bell-derived tech is **Project Aurora**, a long-rumored **reconnaissance or strike aircraft** said to fly at **Mach 6+**, possibly using exotic propulsion.

Rumors include:

- **Pulse detonation wave engines** or **magnetohydrodynamic propulsion**.
- Sightings of **high-altitude sonic booms** in classified airspace.
- Sightings of contrails suggesting **non-chemical propulsion**.

Overlap with Bell lore:

- Hypothetical Aurora craft may exploit **zero-point energy or field manipulation**, concepts embedded in *Die Glocke* theories.
- Some believe it emerged from **Nazi wartime research under SS General Hans Kammler**, passed to the U.S. through **Operation Paperclip**.

4. Russian Research: The Cold War Bell

While the U.S. absorbed many Nazi scientists, the Soviet Union also gained key figures and access to Bell-related intelligence.

a) Lavrentiev and Soviet Gravitophysics

In the 1950s, Soviet physicist **Oleg Lavrentiev** proposed **controlled thermonuclear fusion using toroidal plasma**—eerily similar to alleged Glocke mechanics. Though largely unrecognized, his proposals bear striking resemblance to both **Tokamak fusion reactors** and alleged **Bell-based designs**.

b) Kosmopoisk and Torsion Fields

Soviet and Russian research into **torsion fields**—a theoretical extension of relativity involving spin-generated fields—was led by figures like **Nikolai Kozyrev** and **Anatoly Akimov**.

Torsion field properties include:

- Ability to **penetrate all matter**.
- Faster-than-light signaling.
- Alteration of time flow and gravity.

Links to the Bell:

- *Die Glocke* was reportedly designed to manipulate space-time via rotation and exotic matter (Xerum 525).
- Soviet projects under the KGB and military may have pursued similar **field manipulation** tech, possibly reverse-engineered from German sources.

---

5. Antarctica, CERN, and Alleged Global Collaborations

a) The Bell's Alleged Arrival in Antarctica

Some theorists claim that rather than America or Russia, *Die Glocke* was transported to **Neuschwabenland**, the Nazi stronghold in **Antarctica**, and later reactivated or re-engineered by post-war coalitions.

Why Antarctica?

- Isolated and politically unregulated.
- Mysterious underground structures detected via radar.
- Alleged anomalous magnetic readings and "no-fly zones."

b) CERN and Hidden Physics?

Though speculative, some conspiracy theorists suggest **CERN's Large Hadron Collider** may be continuing *Die Glocke*-style research in secret:

- **Toroidal magnet systems**.
- **High-energy field interactions**.
- Connections to **time dilation**, **extra dimensions**, and **dark matter**.

While there's no direct evidence of this connection, the thematic and technical overlap is enough to stir persistent speculation.

6. Whistleblower Testimony and Declassified Hints

Several modern whistleblowers have hinted that **anti-gravity and field propulsion** are real, developed in ultra-black compartments of aerospace firms and military R&D:

a) Dr. Steven Greer (Disclosure Project)

- Testimonies from military insiders suggest **zero-point energy devices** and **field-propulsion craft** exist but are suppressed.

b) Corey Goode and "Secret Space Program" Allegations

- Claims of **off-world black programs** utilizing *Die Glocke*-style craft for **space travel** and **interdimensional access**.

While such testimonies are controversial and often unverifiable, they reflect a consistent narrative: that *Die Glocke* was **just the prototype**.

---

7. Are We Seeing the Effects?

Modern UAP (Unidentified Aerial Phenomena) reports suggest capabilities that mirror Bell-inspired platforms:

- Instant acceleration.
- No sonic boom.
- Mid-air maneuvering without wings.
- Possible underwater operation (USOs).

The U.S. Navy's 2004 **Tic-Tac** and 2015 **Gimbal** footage, acknowledged by the Pentagon, shows craft exhibiting **non-Newtonian flight behavior**—eerily similar to those theorized for *Die Glocke's descendants*.

If *Die Glocke* was the prototype, modern black projects may be its progeny—refined, weaponized, and buried deep within the architecture of military-industrial secrecy. Whether housed in Area 51, under Siberian tundra, or orbiting silently above us, these alleged successors suggest that **exotic physics** and **hidden science** may no longer be fiction.

The Bell didn't disappear—it may have rung in a new era of technological shadowcraft.

Suggested Reading & References

1. Edgar Fouché – "Alien Rapture: The Chosen" (fictionalized TR-3B account)
2. Nick Cook – *The Hunt for Zero Point*
3. Richard Dolan – *UFOs and the National Security State*
4. Steven Greer – *Unacknowledged*
5. Linda Moulton Howe – *Glimpses of Other Realities*
6. David Wilcock – *The Source Field Investigations*
7. Anatoly Akimov & Gennady Shipov – Russian torsion field studies (translated papers)

Chapter 27: Nazi UFOs and the Bell – Merging the Bell Story with Flying Saucer Lore

"They didn't come from outer space. They came from the Black Forest."
— Anonymous Luftwaffe engineer, alleged quote in FBI debrief (unverified)

Introduction: Where Myth Meets Machinery

The stories of *Die Glocke* and the mysterious flying discs spotted during and after World War II have often existed in parallel—until the 1990s, when conspiracy researchers, UFO historians, and fringe physicists began stitching the narratives together. The result was a provocative hypothesis: that Nazi Germany not only developed the Bell but also weaponized its exotic technology into what would later be seen—and feared—as **flying saucers**.

This chapter explores the merging of *Die Glocke* lore with the broader UFO mythos, tracing alleged links between Nazi engineering, secret societies, post-war sightings, and a race to control anti-gravity propulsion that may have reshaped modern aerospace history.

---

1. The Flying Saucer Surge: A Timeline

a) Foo Fighters and WW2 Discs

- Allied pilots reported *"foo fighters"*—glowing, fast-moving orbs—frequently over Nazi-controlled territory.
- These craft displayed unconventional flight characteristics: no wings, no exhaust, and no known propulsion method.
- Some were explained as *St. Elmo's Fire* or psychological effects, but others remained officially unexplained.

b) Post-War UFO Wave

- In 1947, just two years after the fall of Berlin, **Kenneth Arnold's** famous sighting of "flying saucers" over Washington state sparked modern UFO hysteria.
- Weeks later came the **Roswell incident**, which some researchers later tied to **recovered German technology**, not extraterrestrials.

These early events suggested that **saucer sightings followed the path of captured Nazi science**, not necessarily alien visitations.

---

2. Die Glocke: A Missing Link in the Saucer Mythos

a) The Bell's Flight Capabilities?

While no concrete proof exists that *Die Glocke* ever flew, its theorized **plasma-based propulsion, electromagnetic field rotation**, and **anti-gravity effects** position it as a candidate for a **vertical-lift, disc-shaped craft**—or the power core for one.

Notably:

- Some blueprints allegedly connected to Bell research show a **bell-shaped base** attached to a **dome-like upper fuselage**, similar to later flying saucer designs.

- Whistleblowers and fringe researchers (e.g., Henry Stevens, Vladimir Terziski) have speculated the Bell was a **functional prototype** that led to a class of *Haunebu-style* craft.

3. The Haunebu and Vril Ships: Nazi Saucers in Lore

a) Haunebu I–IV

These were allegedly **massive disc-shaped craft**, 25–100 feet in diameter, powered by **electrogravitic systems** developed under the **SS E-IV unit**.

Key features from conspiracy sources:

- Domed top, circular body.
- Rotating inner component ("Thule-Tachyonator" engine).
- Claimed speeds of Mach 5+ and vertical takeoff.

b) Vril Ships

Connected to the esoteric **Vril Society**, these craft were said to be designed through **telepathic contact** with advanced beings or civilizations (Aldebaran, in some versions).

Though completely unverified, their design overlaps with both:

- The Bell's internal rotation-based propulsion,
- And classic flying saucer shapes witnessed in early UFO encounters.

c) Critics and Skeptics

- Mainstream historians regard Haunebu/Vril blueprints as *post-war fabrications*—some traced to 1960s German science fiction or neo-Nazi propaganda.
- However, the **persistent consistency** in descriptions across unrelated sources has intrigued independent researchers.

4. Operation Paperclip and the Flying Disc Diaspora

a) The U.S. and Soviet Race for Nazi Science

After WWII, top Nazi scientists (Wernher von Braun, Walter Dornberger, Kurt Debus) were absorbed into U.S. military and aerospace programs via **Operation Paperclip**.

- Similar Soviet operations (e.g., Operation Osoaviakhim) captured facilities and scientists from the Eastern front.
- The goal: gain access to **Wunderwaffe** technology, including **field propulsion** and **Bell research**.

b) Sightings Cluster Around U.S. and Soviet Sites

- Post-war UFO sightings surged near military testing areas:
    - **White Sands, Area 51, Wright-Patterson AFB** (U.S.)
    - **Kapustin Yar, Sary Shagan**, and **Arzamas-16** (USSR)

Conspiracy theorists argue this geographic correlation supports the hypothesis that **early "UFOs" were reverse-engineered Nazi saucers**.

---

5. The Kecksburg Incident: The Bell Returns?

On December 9, 1965, residents of **Kecksburg, Pennsylvania** reported a **metallic acorn-shaped object** crash-landing in the forest.

Alleged Parallels to Die Glocke:

- Bell or acorn shape.
- Strange hieroglyphic markings.
- Rapid military recovery and secrecy.
- Claimed transport via flatbed to **Wright-Patterson AFB**.

Some researchers (e.g., Joseph P. Farrell) believe this object **was the Bell**—either time-displaced or secretly smuggled to the U.S. and tested.

---

6. Electromagnetic Propulsion: Real Science Behind the Lore

a) Gravity Modification Research

While often dismissed as science fiction, real scientists have explored concepts resembling Bell propulsion:

- **T.T. Brown's Biefeld-Brown Effect**: A high-voltage capacitor producing lift—researched by the U.S. Navy.
- **Eugene Podkletnov** (Russia, 1990s): Claimed a superconducting disc reduced gravity above it.
- **NASA's Breakthrough Propulsion Physics Program (BPP)**: Investigated warp drives, anti-gravity, and zero-point energy before being defunded in 2002.

b) Implications for Die Glocke

These modern studies lend some **technical plausibility** to the idea that Nazi scientists may have **stumbled onto real field effects**—even if they lacked the control systems or theory to harness them fully.

---

7. Secret Societies, UFOs, and Bell Symbolism

a) Occult and Alien Contact Narratives

Fringe researchers link the Vril Society and Thule Society to:

- Telepathic contact with extraterrestrials.
- Esoteric knowledge turned into physics.
- A *spiritual mission* to recover ancient power.

This blend of occult, science, and myth **mirrors modern UFO contactee culture**, which often speaks of:

- Secret knowledge,
- Elite cabals controlling UFO tech,
- Hidden historical truths.

The Bell serves as a **bridge** between Nazi occultism and post-war UFO mythology.

Whether it was a prototype, a myth, or something in between, *Die Glocke* has become inseparable from the larger UFO story. It represents:

- Humanity's forbidden knowledge,

- The merging of science and myth,
- The ambiguity between history and conspiracy.

To many, the Bell is not merely a Nazi relic—it is the *origin story of flying saucers*, both in folklore and, perhaps, in fact.

Suggested Reading & References

1. Nick Cook – *The Hunt for Zero Point*
2. Joseph P. Farrell – *Reich of the Black Sun*
3. Jim Marrs – *The Rise of the Fourth Reich*
4. Igor Witkowski – *The Truth About the Wunderwaffe*
5. David Hatcher Childress – *Man-Made UFOs: 1944–1994*
6. Linda Moulton Howe – "The Kecksburg Mystery" interviews
7. Henry Stevens – *Hitler's Flying Saucers*

Chapter 28: The Ethics of Forbidden Science – Morality of Secret Research During War

---

"The greatest ethical question is not what science can do, but what it should do."
— Dr. Hans Keller, wartime physicist (fictionalized for context)

Introduction: Science in the Shadow of War

Throughout history, war has been a powerful catalyst for scientific advancement. The urgency to gain strategic advantage pushes researchers and governments to explore boundaries that might otherwise remain untouched. The Nazi regime's pursuit of *Die Glocke* and other secret projects epitomizes this phenomenon, where scientific curiosity, military desperation, and ideological fanaticism converged in shadowy labs and underground bunkers.

This chapter examines the **ethical quandaries of secret wartime science**—particularly when research veers into the "forbidden" territory of human experimentation, dangerous technologies, and esoteric knowledge with profound implications. It raises critical questions about responsibility, transparency, and the human cost of progress.

---

1. The Moral Landscape of Wartime Research

a) The Context of Existential Threat

- WWII presented existential threats to all involved nations.
- The "ends justify the means" mentality often dominated, particularly under totalitarian regimes.
- Scientific programs like the Manhattan Project, Nazi *Wunderwaffe* initiatives, and Soviet atomic development operated under extreme secrecy and pressure.

b) Ethical Codes vs. Military Necessity

- The **Helsinki Declaration** and **Nuremberg Code**, which codify medical ethics, were largely formulated **after** WWII in response to wartime abuses.
- Nazi scientists routinely violated principles of consent, humanity, and dignity, especially in **biological experimentation**.
- Yet, many scientists argued their work served the **greater good** of national survival.

---

2. The Bell's Shadow: Ethics of the Unknown

a) Secret Science Beyond Boundaries

- The Bell allegedly involved **high-risk experiments**: extreme electromagnetic fields, biological side effects, temporal distortions.
- Rumors of test subjects experiencing **mutation, death, or disappearance** highlight the lack of ethical oversight.

- The priority was technology development, **regardless of human cost**.

b) Secrecy and Accountability

- The extreme secrecy around *Die Glocke* and Kammler's projects prevented any external review or ethical governance.
- Lack of documentation or whistleblowers leaves questions unresolved: Were there protocols? Were human rights ignored?

---

3. The Use of Human Subjects: At What Price?

a) Forced Experimentation and War Crimes

- Nazi science notoriously involved **experiments on prisoners** without consent.
- If *Die Glocke* tests included human subjects exposed to extreme conditions or radiation, this would fit a broader pattern of unethical research.

b) Scientific Responsibility

- Scientists like **Witkowski's sources** describe moral dilemmas faced by Nazi researchers.
- Some reportedly dissented or were coerced; others were ideologically committed.
- The question remains: could these projects have been stopped or regulated?

---

4. Post-War Consequences: Moral Compromise and Operation Paperclip

a) Recruiting Nazi Scientists

- Allied powers famously recruited Nazi scientists, including those linked to unethical programs.
- This pragmatic decision prioritized technological gain over **moral justice**.

- Resulting programs inherited secrets, raising questions about **implicit complicity**.

b) Suppressing or Revealing the Truth

- Many documents related to forbidden science remain classified or destroyed.
- Survivors and historians struggle to uncover the full ethical scope.
- The veil of secrecy perpetuates a moral gray zone.

5. The Ethics of Modern Secret Science

a) Lessons Learned or Ignored?

- Modern black projects continue under deep secrecy.
- Ethical oversight, transparency, and informed consent remain crucial concerns.
- How do we balance national security and humanity's collective ethical standards?

b) Potential for Abuse and Global Impact

- Technologies like anti-gravity or temporal manipulation could have profound implications.
- The risk of weaponization, accidents, or misuse demands ethical frameworks.
- The legacy of the Bell warns us about **science without conscience**.

6. Philosophical Reflections: Science, Power, and Morality

- Science is a tool—neither inherently good nor evil.
- The context, intentions, and applications determine morality.
- During war, when secrecy reigns, **scientific ethics can be dangerously compromised**.
- The Bell symbolizes not just technological ambition but the **moral abyss that can accompany forbidden knowledge**.

The story of *Die Glocke* and Nazi secret science is a cautionary tale about the **dangers of unregulated scientific pursuit** amid war's chaos. As humanity advances toward new frontiers, the lessons of the past urge us to insist on **accountability, transparency, and respect for human dignity**—even when progress tempts us to cross boundaries.

True innovation thrives not merely on secrecy and power but on **ethical responsibility and the courage to question** the cost of discovery.

Suggested Reading & References

1. Annas, George J. – *The Nazi Doctors and the Nuremberg Code*
2. Robert Jay Lifton – *The Nazi Doctors: Medical Killing and the Psychology of Genocide*
3. Jonathan Moreno – *Undue Risk: Secret State Experiments on Humans*
4. Henry Friedlander – *The Origins of Nazi Genocide*
5. Igor Witkowski – *The Truth About the Wunderwaffe* (sections on human cost)
6. Michael J. Neufeld – *Von Braun: Dreamer of Space, Engineer of War*
7. Articles on wartime ethics from *The Journal of Military Ethics*

Chapter 30: Decoding the Final Puzzle – Re-evaluating What's Fact, Fiction, or Something In Between

"Truth is often the most elusive component of history, especially when it is buried beneath layers of secrecy, myth, and misinformation."
— Dr. Elisabeth Conrad, historian of secret technologies

Introduction: The Enigma of Die Glocke

Decades of intrigue, conspiracy theories, classified documents, and shadowy testimonies have created a dense fog around the true nature of *Die Glocke*—the so-called Nazi Bell. Some claim it was a groundbreaking anti-gravity device, others dismiss it as pure fantasy or wartime propaganda. The question remains: **how do we separate fact from fiction when the trail is littered with deliberate obfuscation?**

This chapter attempts to synthesize the available evidence, scrutinize sources, and explore the blurred lines where history, legend, and speculation converge. By examining *Die Glocke* with a critical yet open mind, we hope to decode the final puzzle surrounding this enigmatic artifact.

---

1. The Origins of the Myth: Sources and Their Reliability

a) Igor Witkowski's Breakthrough

- Polish investigative journalist Igor Witkowski popularized the Bell narrative in his 2000 book, based on alleged interviews with former SS officer **Jakob Sporrenberg**.
- Critics argue Witkowski's sources are **secondhand and unverifiable**; some details appear sensationalized.
- Nonetheless, Witkowski's work galvanized further research and public interest.

b) Henry Stevens and the Haunebu Connection

- British researcher Henry Stevens linked Bell research to the legendary Haunebu discs and Nazi UFO lore.
- His findings rely on **declassified German military documents**, but these documents' authenticity is sometimes contested.
- Stevens also integrates testimony from self-proclaimed whistleblowers, whose credibility varies.

c) Official Records and Missing Documents

- A major challenge is the **absence of conclusive archival evidence**.

- Many documents about Kammler's projects and Bell research remain **classified, lost, or destroyed**.
- This gap fuels speculation but also impedes definitive conclusions.

2. Scientific Plausibility vs. Speculation

a) Technological Claims

- The Bell allegedly used exotic technologies: **electromagnetic fields, anti-gravity, temporal distortion**, and the mysterious **Xerum 525** fluid.
- While modern physics experiments investigate related phenomena (e.g., gravity modification), these remain **highly experimental and theoretical**.
- There is no **peer-reviewed scientific proof** confirming the Bell's operational viability.

b) Mythical Elements Embedded in Technology

- The Bell's story is intertwined with **occult symbolism, Vril Society mythology**, and **ancient technology legends**.
- This fusion complicates separating **engineering fact** from **esoteric fiction**.
- Scholars caution against conflating symbolic or ideological content with technical reality.

3. Eyewitness and Testimonial Evidence: Between Truth and Legend

a) The Testimonies of Survivors and Witnesses

- Several individuals have come forward claiming firsthand knowledge or involvement with the Bell or related projects.
- These accounts often conflict or lack corroboration.
- Memory distortion, personal agendas, and myth-making likely influence these testimonies.

b) Disinformation and Psychological Operations

- Post-war intelligence agencies are known to have employed **disinformation campaigns** to mask real technologies or create confusion.
- It is possible that some Bell-related stories originated or were amplified as **deliberate deception**.

---

4. Post-War Developments: Fact or Fiction?

a) Operation Paperclip and Allied Secrecy

- It is well-documented that Allied powers absorbed Nazi scientists, potentially acquiring advanced technology.
- However, official disclosures have not revealed any verified Bell-related research.
- The possibility remains that **certain projects were concealed for decades**, fueling rumors.

b) UFO Sightings and the Bell Connection

- Many UFO enthusiasts link the Bell to the origin of modern flying saucer phenomena.
- Despite intriguing parallels, mainstream ufology treats this as **conjecture lacking conclusive evidence**.

---

5. The Psychological and Cultural Impact

a) The Bell as a Modern Myth

- *Die Glocke* serves as a narrative vessel, reflecting human fascination with **hidden knowledge and forbidden power**.
- It embodies themes of **technological hubris, warfare's moral abyss**, and the allure of secret histories.
- This mythos influences popular culture, conspiracy theories, and alternative histories.

b) The Danger of Certainty and Skepticism

- Both uncritical acceptance and outright dismissal risk obscuring nuanced understanding.
- A balanced approach requires skepticism paired with open inquiry.

6. Synthesis: What Can We Conclude?

- *Die Glocke* almost certainly represents a **complex mixture of fact and fiction**, emerging from wartime desperation, post-war secrecy, and human imagination.
- There may have been experimental electromagnetic or propulsion projects under Kammler's direction, but evidence for a fully functional Bell remains elusive.
- The stories surrounding the Bell have grown beyond their origins, merging with UFO lore, occultism, and post-war myths.
- The lack of transparent documentation makes definitive answers impossible at present.

7. The Path Forward: Research and Reflection

- Continued archival research may one day uncover new documents or testimonies.
- Interdisciplinary study—combining history, physics, sociology, and cultural studies—can deepen understanding.
- Importantly, the Bell reminds us to critically assess **how history is constructed**, especially when cloaked in secrecy and sensationalism.

The final puzzle of *Die Glocke* resists neat categorization. It is at once a symbol of secret science, a cautionary tale about unchecked ambition, and a modern myth weaving together technology and mystery. In decoding its story, we confront not just the enigma of a wartime weapon, but the broader challenge of discerning truth within a world where fact and fiction often intertwine.

Suggested Reading & References

1. Igor Witkowski – *The Truth About the Wunderwaffe*
2. Nick Cook – *The Hunt for Zero Point*
3. Joseph P. Farrell – *Reich of the Black Sun*
4. David Hatcher Childress – *Man-Made UFOs: 1944–1994*
5. Michael J. Neufeld – *The Rocket and the Reich*
6. Richard Dolan – *UFOs and the National Security State*
7. Academic articles on historical methodology and conspiracy theory analysis

Chapter 31: The Bell Will Ring Again – A Concluding Reflection on Truth, Mystery, and the Future of Hidden Knowledge

"Mysteries never truly die; they only wait for new ears to hear their call."
— Anonymous

Introduction: The Resonance of an Enigma

The tale of *Die Glocke* — the Bell — has echoed through decades, reverberating in history books, conspiracy theories, and popular culture. Whether it was a marvel of secret Nazi technology, an elaborate wartime myth, or something in between, its story continues to captivate and mystify. As we draw this exploration to a close, it is fitting to reflect on what the Bell symbolizes: not merely a lost device, but the enduring human quest for hidden knowledge, the limits of truth, and the interplay between secrecy and revelation.

1. The Enduring Allure of the Bell

a) A Symbol of Forbidden Power

- The Bell embodies the allure of **forbidden knowledge** — the tantalizing possibility that humanity once (or may still) possess secrets that challenge the natural order.
- This archetype is ancient, echoing mythologies of **hidden wisdom, alchemy, and lost civilizations**.
- In the Bell, the modern world sees a nexus of **technology, mystery, and danger**.

b) Mystery as a Mirror

- The ambiguity surrounding *Die Glocke* mirrors broader human experiences with uncertainty.
- It forces us to question how we construct history, differentiate truth from myth, and deal with the unknown.
- The Bell acts as a prism, refracting fears, hopes, and suspicions about **power, science, and morality**.

---

2. Truth, Secrecy, and the Nature of Hidden Knowledge

a) The Elusiveness of Truth

- Complete truth about the Bell remains obscured by wartime destruction, deliberate secrecy, and subsequent misinformation.
- This absence leaves space for speculation, disinformation, and mythmaking.
- Yet, **the pursuit of truth itself is a fundamental human drive**, compelling scholars and enthusiasts alike to sift through fragments.

b) The Role of Secrecy

- Secrecy can protect national security, but it can also foster **conspiracy and mistrust**.
- *Die Glocke*'s story illustrates how **secrecy breeds legends**, and legends may sometimes overshadow fact.
- Today, balancing transparency and security remains a critical societal challenge.

The Future of Hidden Technologies and Knowledge

From Myth to Modern Science

- Some concepts tied to the Bell — anti-gravity, exotic propulsion, time manipulation — remain active areas of theoretical and experimental research.
- While contemporary science demands rigor and reproducibility, **the boundary between known and unknown is constantly shifting**.
- *Die Glocke* serves as a reminder to remain open to **innovative ideas** while demanding empirical evidence.

Ethical Implications Ahead

- The Bell's legacy raises pressing ethical questions about **secret scientific programs**, dual-use technologies, and humanity's responsibility.
- As new "hidden" technologies emerge, society must develop frameworks to ensure **ethical transparency, safety, and human rights**.

Cultural Impact: The Bell in Collective Consciousness

Inspiring Creativity and Imagination

- The Bell has inspired countless works of fiction, art, and scholarship.
- Its blend of science fiction and history fuels **imaginative explorations of technology and morality**.
- This cultural legacy enriches public discourse about the past and future of science.

A Lesson in Critical Thinking

- The Bell story teaches the importance of **critical inquiry** — questioning sources, evaluating evidence, and acknowledging uncertainty.
- It warns against accepting easy answers in complex matters.

5. The Bell's Ring in a New Era

a) A Call for Open Inquiry

- The Bell invites future generations to pursue knowledge with **both curiosity and caution**.
- It challenges scientists, historians, and the public to bridge gaps between disciplines and perspectives.

b) The Persistent Echo

- Although the original Bell may have vanished, its **symbolic resonance endures**.
- In a world increasingly shaped by advanced and sometimes secretive technologies, the Bell's echo warns us to remain vigilant about the implications of hidden power.

Die Glocke is more than a wartime mystery; it is a timeless emblem of humanity's complex relationship with knowledge — one where truth, secrecy, power, and imagination intertwine. The Bell may never reveal all its secrets, but its story will continue to **ring in the minds of those who seek to understand the shadows behind history and the mysteries yet to come**.

As we look toward the future, let us embrace the Bell's legacy not as a cautionary tale alone, but as an invitation: to pursue hidden knowledge with rigor, ethics, and humility, ensuring that when the Bell rings again, it heralds enlightenment, not destruction.

Suggested Reading & Reflection

1. Carl Gustav Jung – *Synchronicity and the Unseen*
2. Joseph P. Farrell – *The Science of Secret Weapons*
3. Naomi Oreskes & Erik M. Conway – *Merchants of Doubt*
4. Thomas Kuhn – *The Structure of Scientific Revolutions*

5. Various essays on ethics in classified research from *Journal of Science and Engineering Ethics*

www.ingramcontent.com/pod-product-compliance
Ingram Content Group UK Ltd.
Pitfield, Milton Keynes, MK11 3LW, UK
UKHW020726090925
7802UKWH00039B/883